The Church Of God In Christ
Presiding Bishop

Bishop Charles E. Blake, Sr.

God's People: Called to Holy Living
Scripture Reference:
2 Corinthians 7:1; Titus 2:11–14; Hebrews 12:14

Order materials today from the Power for Living Series:

Church Of God In Christ Publishing House
806 East Brooks Road, Memphis, Tennessee 38116
P.O. Box 161330, Memphis, Tennessee 38116
Toll Free: 1-877-746-8578 | Fax: (901) 743-1555
Website: www.cogicpublishinghouse.net
Email: sales@cogicpublishinghouse.net

FROM THE PRESIDING BISHOP'S DESK

Greetings to you in the name of the Lord Jesus Christ,

The year of 2020 is a year in which the world has not experienced in over a hundred years. The COVID-19 Pandemic has plagued our cities, our towns, our churches, and our very lives. We have been forced into isolation with our loved ones. But the one thing that I can say that we are learning from this is that our God shows Himself time and time again. I have received numerous testimonies about how those who were afflicted by the Corona Virus walked out of the hospital healed, or they themselves were exposed and the Lord protected them from contracting this terrible virus.

Others are testifying about a growing connection with God that they have never experienced before. While others are testifying about how this has brought their families together. The greatest gift that God can ever give us is that of a Witness. A witness is one who can bring first hand evidence (proof) of events that happened. Witnessing is one of the most important parts of our Call as Christians. In life, many experience one call and that is the call God makes to the heart for Salvation. Yet there is another call that takes place after we have matured, developed, and grown in the knowledge of the Lord and that is the call to ministry.

One does not have to adorn a title to be called into ministry. In fact, the title Christian itself places upon you the ministry of Christ Jesus. That ministry is witnessing to the hurt, the poor, and to the hungry. That ministry of doing unto others as you would have them do unto you. Sharing the Good News of Salvation; how it has changed your life, and to those who do not know Him. Too many times we become so wrapped up in titles, that we have left the basic principal of our calling; and that is to spread the Gospel of Jesus Christ, to enlarge the kingdom of God. I can tell you that the title of brother or sister is all that you shall ever need to accomplish that.

My brothers and my sisters, this moment in our lives is more than just a moment. It is a movement, and it is a special time to separate the workers from the bench warmers. The Christmas Season is upon us and we as Christians must spread more good tidings to all our friends and family; warm their hearts with merriment of your witness. We may not know what 2021 holds for us, but what I can say is "God shall ALWAYS be with us." Hebrews 13:5 "I will never leave thee, nor forsake thee." That is our witness, that is our call, and that is what we can take with us into 2021.

Merry Christmas Everyone, and a Blessed New Year.

Bishop Charles E. Blake, Sr.
Seventh in Succession
Church Of God In Christ, Inc.

FROM THE CHAIRMAN OF THE PUBLISHING BOARD

Greetings to you in the name of Jesus,

The Christmas Season is upon us, and it is in these moments that we normally reflect on the birth of Jesus Christ. How the Savior was given to us so that one day he would step on the neck of Satan and sacrifice his sinless life for us so that we would be free from the bondage of sin and death. Yet I would like to add that this is a time of reflection and a time of sharing our witness to those who do not know Him.

We have been called without titles! We accepted Christ into our hearts, sharing God's Gospel, the love, and joy that would warm every unbeliever's heart. We have been blindsided by what 2020 has brought us: a pandemic, social injustice, and political turmoil. But while we try to process these unforeseen events, we cannot forget that WE owe this to God. For the Bible says that we were bought with a price, and that price is Jesus Christ. We cannot forget how He bled for our sins and how He endured pain to lift our burdens. Amid pain, suffering, and even death, He never took his focus off of His Father's work.

In 2020, our world has drastically changed. Things will never be as they once were. Yet, we cannot allow what continues to happen in 2020 and in 2021 to take our focus off of our Father's Work. We were called when we accepted the title and the responsibility of a Christian. It is our biblical duty to work out our Father's plan for our lives and the lives of others. Understanding that the plan at times might be difficult, but a song that we sing says "And we'll understand it better by and by."

Our goal is to make this world better, not bitter. As children of God, we must spread hope and not hate. A writer once said, "absence makes the heart grow fonder." Hopefully, in this time apart from one another we have learned how to forgive those who have hurt us and who have left us. This is our chance to become stronger, to become better people as followers of Christ. That my brothers and sisters are the reason for this season, to reflect, to accept, to forgive, and to heal.

Merry Christmas and Happy New Year,
Elder Uleses Henderson, Jr.
Chairman of the Publishing Board

QUARTERLY FOCUS

Dear Sunday School Student,

I would like to thank you for your loyal support of your Publishing House. Due to the COVID-19 Pandemic, we are seeing a time of sorrow and misery never before experienced in most of our lifetimes. With most of us not allowed to worship in our church facility, our Sunday school literature is the perfect source for developing a Bible class in our living rooms. I want to encourage all teachers to ask God to give you a special anointing to speak a word of faith and hope at a time such as this.

This quarter begins by showing the plan of God to bring Salvation to the world through one family line. Creating a people through Abraham; establishing a nation through David; and giving all of humanity, those who are willing to be a part, eternal life through Jesus Christ is truly marvelous. We may not know our ancestral roots in Africa, but we can claim who we our spiritually through the Word of God.

The quarter also teaches how happy the enemy is to bring separation among the Saints. Be-lievers must work to bring healing and reconciliation in the area of racial, cultural, and religious division. Just as the Magi was permitted to come to Jesus and worship him, we should show special hospitality when other cultures attend our service.

The invitation to become fishers of men that Christ gave the disciples, is a reminder that all of us should think of a way that our secular occupation can also be a means by which we can win souls. Maybe the construction supervisor who makes his living building houses, might want to use some of that wisdom as he shows people how to rebuild their lives. As Jesus said follow me and I will make you fishers of men, maybe the carpenter can think of how he can help people rebuild their families.

This quarter places a special emphasis on the power and importance of intercessory prayer. Many of the problems in our community would be solved if people not only prayed for themselves but collectively came together to intercede on behalf of others who may not belong to their particular group. People should realize the blessing they enjoy is because somebody prayed for them.

And finally, this quarter closes with our attention to Lydia. She was not a preacher, or of some high rank in the early Church, her calling and anointing was with hospitality. She was outstanding at finding and providing food and shelter for the needy. We too should want to add the ministry of hospitality to what we do for God.

It is my prayer that you will be wonderfully blessed as you study the Power For Living series for December 2020 through February 2021.

Until the next time,
Bishop J. L. Whitehead, Jr. B.A., M.Div., COGIC Liason
Review team: Dr Alonzo Johnson, Evangelist Irether Sanford, Dr. Goldie Wells, Dr. Avery Brown, Bishop David Hall, and Dr. Adrienne Israel

ADULT QUARTERLY

WINTER QUARTER 2020-2021

DECEMBER 2020 • JANUARY • FEBRUARY 2021

Unit 1 •

December 6	Called Through Heritage	13
December 13	Called Before Birth	24
December 20	A Regal Response to Holy Light	33
December 27	Called to Prepare the Way	42

Unit 2 •

January 3	Called to Proclaim	52
January 10	Called to Significance	61
January 17	Called to Heal	69
January 24	Called as the Intercessor	78
January 31	Prophesying Daughters	87

Unit 3 •

February 7	Called to Evangelize	95
February 14	Mary Magdalene: A Faithful Disciple	104
February 21	Priscilla: Called to Minister	112
February 28	Lydia: Called to Serve	123

Special Features: Teaching Tips and Ideas, Quarterly Quiz

Bishop Charles E. Blake, Sr.
Seventh in Succession
Church Of God In Christ, Inc.

Elder Uleses Henderson Jr., Esq.
Chairman, Publishing Board
Church Of God In Christ, Inc.

TEACHING TIPS AND IDEAS

TIP #1

We as teachers of Sunday School have to remain encouraged, focused and inspired to make a difference in another person's life, be it a child or adult (1 Samuel 30:6).

TIP #2

Some of us will not have mega Sunday Schools as far as the number of people who will show up for class, but that should not be our focus. We should prepare and study just as diligently to teach five students, as we would to teach 100.

Remember to always pray for your Sunday School class and your preparation. Study your lessons (subject matter) thoroughly; do research and be prepared to teach. Don't let being "right", be your main objective, but be open minded to entertain other perspectives, as long as they are in line with the Word. Our lessons should be relevant and interesting. We must be faithful to God and to the call of teaching! So teach your class as if your life depended on it; and it does, your eternal life.

TIP #3

We should be excited to share with others what God has given to us. We must not be stingy or selfish with our talents. We should not have to be begged to do a work for God. Be willing to use our gifts and talents to further the kingdom of God through Sunday School. We will not hide or bury our talents (Matthew 25:15-30). God didn't bless us with what we have just to sit on and not give it out to the world.

When we are asked to do something, we should not say "why me?" But "why not me?"

TIP #4

To help keep your class exciting, especially for the younger groups, we can change the scenery or program from the usual. You can take your class outside the church or sanctuary. You can go to the park, etc. If your younger students are not attending class on Sunday morning, you

may need to move it to another time or day to accommodate them. You may incorporate Christian movies/videos, music, games, and crafts to enhance your teaching. You can do role play and skits with your younger students (play acting) as a bible character, etc.

TIP #5

Always be prompt; start your class at the appointed time. When a student who tends to be habitually late, finds out that the class will start on time, they may have a tendency to make a special effort to get to the class on time.

TIP #6

Always sing a song, preferably a Sunday School song, during the session.

TIP #7

Learn the personality of each student. Some love to be called out to participate; some do not like to participate, e.g., reading aloud. Be prayerful in how to wisely treat your individual student.

TIP #8

There are many resources and ideas online, etc, e.g., Sunday School Center. You can get various materials for Easter and other themes to make your classroom experience exciting. Listen and be open to receive ideas from others. Be grateful that you are making a difference in the lives of your students.

YOUR PURPOSE FULFILLED

Once a person gives themselves to Jesus and becomes a new creature, they have a dire need to learn the Word of God and how to apply it to their lives. Sunday School is the excellent place and opportunity to accomplish this.

We continue to pray for teachers worldwide and you in particular.

QUARTERLY QUIZ

These questions may be used in two ways: as a pretest at the beginning of the quarter; as a review at the end of the quarter; or as a review after each lesson. Questions are based on the Scripture text of each lesson (King James Version).

LESSON 1

1. Why is Matthew's record of Jesus' lineage an indication of the audience to whom he is writing?

_____

_____

2. Make an outline contrasting why Jesus is better than angels according to Hebrews 1:1–5.

_____

_____

LESSON 2

1. Why did the angel address Joseph as "son of David" in Matthew 1:20?

_____

_____

2. Why is Joseph's obedience instructive? What do we learn?

_____

_____

LESSON 3

1. Since the wise men follow the stars (Matthew 2:9), why is it wrong for believers today to check their horoscopes?

_____

_____

2. Why is it culturally significant that Jesus spent part of his childhood in Egypt (Matthew 2:14)?

_____

_____

LESSON 4

1. Why is repentance—having a changed mind— evident in a changed lifestyle (Matthew 3:2)?

_____

_____

2. John the Baptist was bold in confronting the religious leaders of his day. Why is this instructive for us today?

_____

_____

LESSON 5

1. Luke 4:14–17 says Jesus' ministry was initiated after sacrifice and obedience.

_____

_____

2. Why is the Holy Ghost essential for ministry?

_____

_____

QUARTERLY QUIZ

LESSON 6

1. Why is Simon's obedience to go fishing again in Luke 5:5 a demonstration of his faith?

_____

_____

2. Why did Jesus use the analogy in Luke 5:10 that Simon will now be a fisher of men?

_____

_____

LESSON 7

1. In the face of an obstacle like the closed door in Mark 2:1–4, why is the four friends' creativity encouraging?

_____

_____

2. Why is it wise to have friends who are full of faith?

_____

_____

LESSON 8

1. What emotions do you sense as Jesus is praying the High Priestly Prayer in John 17:14–24?

_____

_____

2. Why does Jesus pray the disciples will be sanctified?

_____

_____

LESSON 9

1. Why does the Gospel writer, Luke, include the prophetess Anna in accounting the events surrounding the Messiah's birth?

_____

_____

2. Why is it significant that Joel's prophesy in Acts 2:16–17 explicitly mentions women?

_____

_____

LESSON 10

1. In John 4:25–30, why was the Samaritan woman so responsive to the fact that Jesus was the Messiah?

_____

_____

2. Why are the metaphors of water (Samaritan woman) and food (John 4:32) helpful in describing spiritual needs?

_____

_____

QUARTERLY QUIZ

LESSON 11

1.Why does the writer record the names of the women who are at the cross and at the tomb in Mark 15:40?

_____

_____

2. Why is it so beautiful that Jesus calls Mary's name in John 20:16?

_____

_____

LESSON 12

1. Why is teamwork and partnership vital to ministry success as demonstrated by Paul, Priscilla, and Aquila in Acts 18:18–21?

_____

_____

2. Why are Priscilla and Aquila courageous in correcting Apollos?

_____

_____

LESSON 13

1. In Acts 16:13 God directed Paul and his team to join the women's worship service at the river. Why is this significant?

_____

_____

2. In Acts 16:13 God directed Paul and his team to join the women's worship service at the river. Why is this significant?

_____

_____

DECEMBER 2020 • JANUARY • FEBRUARY 2021

Lesson 1
1. The list highlights Jesus' Jewish ancestry. Matthew is writing this Gospel or "Good News" to the Jews.
2. Jesus is better than the angels because: 1. God created angels; Jesus is God and He was active in creation. 2. Angels respond to God to intercede for humans; As God the Son, Jesus sits at the right hand of the Father interceding for us. 3. Angels are named by God; Jesus has a name, which is above the name of angels.

Lesson 2
1. The angel reminded Joseph of his lineage to the Messiah.
2. Joseph obeyed as soon as he woke up from his dream. We learn to obey God immediately.

Lesson 3
1. The Bible makes it very clear that the study of horoscopes is sin (Deuteronomy 4:19).
2. Egypt is on the continent of Africa. God is inclusive of people of color who are rejected by so many. Answers will vary.

Lesson 4
1. With a changed mind, the one who repents turns away from sin and goes in the opposite direction. Being sorry is not the same as repentance. To repent means to stop, consider, and change the behavior.
2. Answers will vary.

Lesson 5
1. Answers will vary.
2. Answers will vary.

Lesson 6
1. Obedience—without seeing or understanding the outcome—is an act of faith. Answers will vary.
2. As a fisherman, Simon could relate to this analogy or word picture. He knew how to catch fish. Now he is beginning to understand that he has a new role—"catching" men to follow Jesus.

ANSWERS TO QUARTERLY QUIZ

DECEMBER 2020 • JANUARY • FEBRUARY 2021

Lesson 7
1. Answers will vary.
1. Answers will vary.

Lesson 8
1. Answers will vary.
2. The disciples have much work to do in spreading the Gospel. They have been set apart for this task.

Lesson 9
1. Luke recognizes God's faithfulness to Anna.
2. Women are in God's plan to be used by Him. Answers will vary.

Lesson 10
1. The encounter with Jesus changed her life. Answers will vary.
2. We all need water and food to survive. Satisfying spiritual thirst and hunger is essential to growing spiritually.

Lesson 11
1. The writer demonstrates that women remained faithful to Jesus and were a significant part of His ministry.
2. God knows the name of each part of His creation (Isaiah 40:26). He knows the secret name of every follower who overcomes (Revelation 2:17). He knows Mary's name. He sees her. And He knows our names.

Lesson 12
1. Answers will vary.
2. It takes courage to correct someone.

Lesson 13
1. Women are integral—not incidental—to the Church.
2. The women were able to follow the ritual of washing before prayer.

CALLED THROUGH HERITAGE

BIBLE BASIS: Matthew 1:1–6, 16–17; Hebrews 1:1–5

BIBLE TRUTH: The humanity and deity of Christ are affirmed in Jesus' lineage.

MEMORY VERSE: "[God] hath in these last days spoken unto us by his Son, whom he hath appointed heir of all things, by whom also he made the worlds" (Hebrews 1:2, KJV).

LESSON AIM: By the end of this lesson, we will EVALUATE the significance of Jesus' earthly heritage and His heavenly origins, WONDER at the depth and scope of God's eternal plan to bring salvation through Jesus, and WORSHIP Jesus as God's definitive word to humanity.

BACKGROUND SCRIPTURES: Matthew 1:1–17; Hebrews 1—Read and incorporate the insights gained from the Background Scriptures into your study of the lesson.

TEACHER PREPARATION

MATERIALS NEEDED: Bibles (several different versions), Quarterly Commentary/Teacher Manual, Adult Quarterly, teaching resources such as charts, worksheets/handouts, paper, pens, pencils

OTHER MATERIALS NEEDED / TEACHER'S NOTES:

_____

_____

LESSON OVERVIEW

LIFE NEED FOR TODAY'S LESSON
Where we come from often speaks volumes about what we are like. How are people rooted in what has come before? Hebrews affirms the ultimate origins of Jesus in the very life of God, and Matthew explains how He was the product of His long biblical heritage.

BIBLE LEARNING
Jesus is fully God and fully man.

BIBLE APPLICATION
Christians celebrate the humanity and deity of Jesus Christ, the Savior of the world, and our High Priest.

STUDENTS' RESPONSES
Believers recognize that Jesus, the Messiah, is prophet, priest, and king.

LESSON SCRIPTURE

MATTHEW 1:1-6, 16-17, KJV

1 The book of the generation of Jesus Christ, the son of David, the son of Abraham.

2 Abraham begat Isaac; and Isaac begat Jacob; and Jacob begat Judas and his brethren;

3 And Judas begat Phares and Zara of Thamar; and Phares begat Esrom; and Esrom begat Aram;

4 And Aram begat Aminadab; and Aminadab begat Naasson; and Naasson begat Salmon;

5 And Salmon begat Booz of Rachab; and Booz begat Obed of Ruth; and Obed begat Jesse;

6 And Jesse begat David the king; and David the king begat Solomon of her that had been the wife of Urias;

16 And Jacob begat Joseph the husband of Mary, of whom was born Jesus, who is called Christ.

17 So all the generations from Abraham to David are fourteen generations; and from David until the carrying away into Babylon are fourteen generations; and from the carrying away into Babylon unto Christ are fourteen generations.

Hebrews 1:1 God, who at sundry times and in divers manners spake in time past unto the fathers by the prophets,

2 Hath in these last days spoken unto us by his Son, whom he hath appointed heir of all things, by whom also he made the worlds;

3 Who being the brightness of his glory, and the express image of his person, and upholding all things by the word of his power, when he had by himself purged our sins, sat down on the right hand of the Majesty on high:

4 Being made so much better than the angels, as he hath by inheritance obtained a more excellent name than they.

5 For unto which of the angels said he at any time, Thou art my Son, this day have I begotten thee? And again, I will be to him a Father, and he shall be to me a Son?

BIBLICAL DEFINITIONS

A. Begat (**Matthew 1:2**) *gennao* (Gk.)—To be the father of, by direct parentage or ancestral ties

B. Express Image (**Hebrews 1:3**) *charakter* (Gk.)—A stamp or imprint left by a seal on sealing wax; a replica

LIGHT ON THE WORD

Joseph and Mary. Both of Jesus' earthly parents were descendants of King David. Joseph was Jesus' earthly and legal father—though not His biological father—who was engaged to Mary when Jesus was conceived by the Holy Ghost. Joseph was a righteous man (**Matthew 1:19**), meaning he had spiritual discernment and was sensitive to the guidance of the Lord, regardless of the consequences. Mary was chosen by God to carry, bear, and raise the Savior of the world. The couple had children together after Jesus' birth.

Genealogical Lists. Bible genealogies, though cumbersome for the modern reader, are essential for the worldview of the Bible's original audiences. The lists let the audience feel the weight of the incredible span of years through which God has been working His plan of cultivating a people for Himself. Genealogies link Scriptural stories to a verifiable history of people. The term "begat" or "fathered" denotes an ancestor, not necessarily a direct, biological parent

14

(1 Kings 15:11; 2 Kings 18:3; 22:2). In so doing, the author streamlines the account. The ancestors are highlighted who are relevant to the author's purpose in writing.

TEACHING THE BIBLE LESSON

LIFE NEED FOR TODAY'S LESSON

AIM: Students will agree that Jesus is the Son of God.

INTRODUCTION

Lord and Savior

The Gospels are about the birth, life, death, and resurrection of our Savior. The Old Testament, in its entirety, lays the groundwork for the Messiah. It is a bridge connecting the humanness of Jesus, the son of Mary and Joseph, to the supernatural Christ the King, the Son of God. Delving into the human genealogy of Christ far surpasses the mystery of uncovering our family ancestry. As we search name by name from Abraham, to Boaz, to Solomon, we realize that all the pieces fit together and give us a perfect picture of Christ.

The original readers of the Letter to the Hebrews faced a dilemma. As Jews, they practiced Judaism all their lives. When the apostles and other Christian believers presented the Good News of salvation to them, many turned to Christ as Lord and Savior. However, some were beginning to wonder how an unknown son of a carpenter from an obscure village called Nazareth could be greater than their forefathers or the prophets like Moses. The author reminds these believers of the essential truth of their new faith, demonstrating that Jesus Christ is superior to all others because He was born of God.

BIBLE LEARNING

AIM: Students will analyze the ancestry of Jesus Christ.

I. JESUS' DIVERSE ANCESTRY (MATTHEW 1:1–6)

Matthew begins by summarizing that Jesus is descended from Abraham and David. God made a covenant with Abraham that from his lineage all the earth would be blessed (Genesis 12:3). God also promised David that an eternal King would come from his seed (Psalm 89:3–4). This King and global blessing is Jesus Christ.

While establishing Christ as the heir of the covenant and the throne, Matthew's genealogy also refuses to hide the sinners and Gentiles in Jesus' family tree. Tamar resorted to prostitution to force her father-in-law Judah to fulfill his promise of a child through his family. The twins, Perez and Zerah, the result of that union, have their place in Christ's lineage (Genesis 38). The Canaanite Rahab was a pagan and perhaps a prostitute (Joshua 2:11), but she heard of God's awesome power and decided to join God's people. Rahab's son Boaz married Ruth, a foreigner who became a faithful follower of God. Even the great King Solomon was born from a marriage that began with deceit and murder (2 Samuel 11:2–17).

Matthew 1:1 The book of the generation of Jesus Christ, the son of David, the son of Abraham.

From the fourth word of his Gospel, Matthew clearly asserts that Jesus is the Christ. "Christ" (Gk. *Christos*, **KHREES**-toce) in Hebrew is "Messiah" (*mashiyach*, maw-**SHEE**-akh). Both titles mean "anointed." In the Old Testament, the term anointed is frequently applied to kings and priests and sometimes to prophets. Jesus Christ fulfilled all three functions of king, priest, and prophet.

Jesus was "the son of David, the son of Abraham" (**Matthew 1:1**). David and Abraham are the two most prominent names in Jesus' genealogy. David's name shows that Jesus is of royal descent and the Messiah (see **9:27**; **Acts 2:30**). Jews consider "son of David" as a messianic title (**Isaiah 9:7**). Abraham's name points to Jesus' Jewish origin (**Genesis 22:18**). With these first words, Matthew presents Jesus as the Messiah directly descended from the royal house of David and the seed of the patriarch Abraham, to whom God gave the divine promises.

2 Abraham begat Isaac; and Isaac begat Jacob; and Jacob begat Judas and his brethren;

Matthew's genealogy begins with Abraham through whom God promised to bless all nations. While Luke traces Jesus' genealogy to Adam (**Luke 3:38**) to show Christ's authority over all humanity, Matthew is more interested in highlighting Jesus' heritage. Abraham's faith withstood much testing (**Hebrews 11:17–19**). Abraham is called "the Friend of God" (**James 2:23**), "faithful" (**Galatians 3:9**), and "the father of us all" (**Romans 4:16**). Abraham was declared by God to be the father of a multitude and called by God for the specific purpose of blessing the world (**Genesis 12:2-3, 7**).

Abraham's son, Isaac, is a type of Christ because he was a child of promise. Also, like Christ, Issac was to be sacrificed by his father. However, when God saw Abraham's willingness to obey, Issac's life was spared.

One of Isaac's sons, Jacob (later renamed Israel), was the heir of the promise while he was still inside the womb (**Genesis 25:23**). God's grace chose him over his older twin brother, Esau. Matthew lists Jacob as Jesus' earthly ancestor. "Judas" is the Greek spelling of "Judah" (AMP), one of Jacob's sons. This ancestors' list is not an exhaustive inventory of Jesus' family tree.

3 And Judas begat Phares and Zara of Thamar; and Phares begat Esrom; and Esrom begat Aram;

Judah was the fourth son of Jacob and Leah. Judah participated in the plot to kill his brother Joseph, but later Judah intervened to save Joseph's life by suggesting that his brothers sell Joseph into slavery instead (**Genesis 37:26-27**). Judah took the lead in the affairs of the family and was given a blessing of leadership by his father Jacob (**Genesis 46:28**; **49:8-12**). Judah resided among the Canaanites at Adullam for a time and married a Canaanite woman.

Judah's son Er also married a Canaanite woman named Tamar (Greek spelling: Thamar). Er died prematurely (**Genesis 38:1–7**), and although Judah had his second son marry Tamar to provide her with an heir, his second son also died. Judah withheld his third son from Tamar, caring more for his heir than for his twice-widowed daughter-in-law. Tamar, in turn, stooped to posing as a prostitute and slept with Judah to gain progeny. The twin sons born to Tamar were named Perez and Zerah (Greek spelling: Phares and Zara), one of whom, Phares, became an ancestor of the Messiah.

4 And Aram begat Aminadab; and Aminadab begat Naasson; and Naasson begat Salmon; 5 And Salmon

16

begat Booz of Rachab; and Booz begat Obed of Ruth; and Obed begat Jesse;

Aram is not mentioned outside of genealogical lists, but "Nahshon son of Amminadab" is one of the leaders of Israel in the wilderness (**Numbers 1:7**). We also find these names in the genealogies of David and Moses (**Ruth 4:19**; **Exodus 6:23** respectively).

Like Judah, Nahshon's son Salmon enters an inter-ethnic marriage. God prohibited His people from marrying outsiders because of religious affiliation. Rahab (Greek spelling: Rachab) had faith in the God who delivered the Hebrews from Pharaoh, which led her to assist Joshua in his conquest of Jericho (**Joshua 2-6**). In return for her help, Joshua spared Rahab and her household when the Israelites destroyed Jericho (**Joshua 6:17-25**). Because of her faith in Yahweh, Rahab was naturalized into the people of God and married Salmon. Rahab is one of the "sheroes" of faith (**Hebrews 11:31**).

Boaz, whom we know from the book of Ruth, was the son of Salmon and Rahab. Boaz was a wealthy relative of Naomi's deceased husband. When Naomi returned to her homeland after the death of her husband, her daughter-in-law, Ruth, went with her. Ruth had to glean grain in the fields to provide food for her mother-in-law and herself. In the process, Ruth met Boaz, who showed her favor by instructing his workers to leave extra grain for Ruth to glean. Naomi took notice, and in line with the customs of her people, Naomi instructed Ruth to lie down at Boaz's feet to show that Boaz was responsible for her care. Boaz married Ruth and became her kinsman-redeemer. From this union with

yet another outsider was born, a son named Obed, who had a son named Jesse.

6 And Jesse begat David the king; and David the king begat Solomon of her that had been the wife of Urias;

Jesse had seven sons and two daughters (**2 Chronicles 2:13-16**), but of all these children, only David is mentioned in this list. David was chosen by God through the prophet and received the promise of a royal Messiah in his lineage. The addition of "the king" (Gk. *basileus*, bah-see-**LAY**-ooce) emphasizes the imperial importance of Jesus' ancestry.

SEARCH THE SCRIPTURES

QUESTION 1
Why is Matthew's record of Jesus' lineage an indication of the audience to whom he is writing?

The list highlights Jesus' Jewish ancestry. Matthew is writing this Gospel, or "Good News," to the Jews.

QUESTION 2
In what ways has God redeemed the negative parts of your family history and made them into something beautiful?

Answers will vary.

LIGHT ON THE WORD

Four Women
A curious characteristic of the list of Jesus' ancestors is the mention of four women: Tamar (**v. 3**), Rahab (**v. 5**), Ruth (**v. 5**), and "the wife of Uriah" (**v. 6**). Women's names seldom appear in Jewish genealogies, yet these four are prominent.

Tamar, Rahab, and Ruth were Gentiles. Tamar posed as a prostitute; Rahab's profession was a prostitute; Ruth was from the idolatrous nation of Moab; and, Bathsheba was an adulterer. Still, Matthew includes these four women in the genealogy. Their lives are lessons about the universality of the Gospel, the grace of God toward humanity, and reminders that the blood of Jesus Christ cleanses every sin. God's redemptive plan is for anyone who receives Jesus as Lord and Savior (**Romans 10:9–10**).

II. JESUS' PLACE IN HISTORY (vv. 16–17)

While Joseph was the man who reared Jesus, he is not Jesus' biological father. Nevertheless, Jesus was heir to the genealogical history of Joseph's earthly ancestry.

In his genealogy, Matthew grounds Jesus in Jewish history. Abraham was the Father of the Faith. David was the king of the promise. During the period of the Babylonian exile, there was loss of life and the destruction of the Temple, which represented God's presence. Just as fourteen generations passed between each of these significant events in Jewish history, now fourteen more generations have passed since the exile. In this presentation of lineage, Matthew shows the progression of God's plan in salvation history.

16 And Jacob begat Joseph the husband of Mary, of whom was born Jesus, who is called Christ. 17 So all the generations from Abraham to David are fourteen generations; and from David until the carrying away into Babylon are fourteen generations; and from the carrying away into Babylon unto Christ are fourteen generations.

From David and Solomon, Matthew lists the kings of Israel and Judah until the fall to Babylon and exile, then from the exile to Jesus. Matthew affirms the Jewishness of this genealogy by referencing the numbers of generations. Fourteen is significant because it is seven twice, and seven is the number of completion. His point is that the timing of Jesus' birth fits perfectly with the whole of God's plan since He first called Abraham's descendants to be His people. Matthew lists three sets of fourteen generations before the Messiah, and three is a number showing divinity and completion. Matthew excluded four kings of Israel (Ahaziah, Joash, Amaziah, and Jehoiakim) to reach the number fourteen between David and the exile. The word "begat" (Gk. *gennao*, genn-**NAH**-oh) denotes ancestral linkage, without necessarily implying direct parentage. Matthew would expect his audience to know the line of kings of Judah. Otherwise, he would not place them so prominently in his Gospel.

SEARCH THE SCRIPTURES

QUESTION 3
Matthew's genealogy emphasizes the Jewishness of Jesus. How would you present your genealogy to emphasize your ethnicity?

Answers will vary.

QUESTION 4
Are you able to trace the genealogy of your faith through those who led you to salvation?

Answers will vary.

LIGHT ON THE WORD

The Courage of Joseph
God the Father entrusted Jesus to an earthly dad, Joseph. While Mary is rightly

celebrated, without a husband to protect her and her child, it would have been nearly impossible for Mary to navigate, considering the circumstances of her day. Joseph was courageous. Amid the air of scandal, he married Mary and became a father to her son. Joseph's role in caring for his family is truly heroic, and Matthew honors him by including Joseph's lineage in Jesus' family tree.

Today, many courageous men become fathers to children whom they have not sired. These dads assume the physical, emotional, and financial responsibility to raise and protect children, which provides them with a solid foundation for the future. Let's celebrate fathers who willingly step in to shelter and support sons and daughters who might not otherwise know what it means to have a dad.

3. JESUS' TRUE HERITAGE (HEBREWS 1:1-5)

While Matthew communicates Jesus' humanness through His earthly father's genealogy, the writer of Hebrews affirms Jesus' divinity through His Heavenly Father. To support this argument, the author turns to Scripture. He first quotes from a messianic psalm (**Psalm 2:7**). While this psalm's promise was already metaphorically fulfilled in the reigns of David and Solomon, the promise finds its full, literal completion in Jesus. The second quote likewise is initially, partially fulfilled in Solomon (**2 Samuel 7:14**). God's covenant with David promised that David's "son" would be an eternal king over God's people. Solomon inherited these blessings but ultimately failed to live up to God's standard. As later prophesied, David's "son," Jesus—who was born in the lineage

of David—demonstrated faithfulness through His life and death. As prophesied, Jesus inherited the blessings of the Davidic covenant. The idea of inheritance (**v. 4**) is a crucial concept in Hebrews. Since Jesus is the Son of God, He is able to pass an eternal inheritance to those who follow Him.

Hebrews 1:1 God, who at sundry times and in divers manners spake in time past unto the fathers by the prophets, 2 Hath in these last days spoken unto us by his Son, whom he hath appointed heir of all things, by whom also he made the worlds;

The letter of Hebrews begins with God as the subject. The writer's perspective is noticeably God-centered. He is the omnipresent God who intervened in human history with His sovereign Word addressed to humankind. However, His ultimate Word was One who has a unique relationship with God.

As opposed to a full revelation of His Word, the word "sundry" refers to the gradual uncovering of the mind and the will of God, who revealed His intent through the prophets. "In divers manners" refers to the various methods of communication. In the time of the forefathers, God spoke to Moses in the burning bush (**Exodus 3:2 ff.**); to Elijah, God spoke in a still, small voice (**1 Kings 19:12 ff.**); to Isaiah, God spoke in a vision in the Temple (**Isaiah 6:1 ff.**); to Hosea, God spoke through his family circumstances (**Hosea 1:2**); and to Amos, God spoke through a basket of summer fruit (**Amos 8:1**). Now, God is speaking to us in the language of His "Son," literally the new language of Christ. Christ is the Word of God.

Jesus' divine nature makes Him the right and only capable bearer of God's complete revelation. Jesus is more than a prophet. Jesus Christ alone brings to humanity the full revelation of God. First, Jesus has been "appointed heir of all things." The word "heir" (Gk. *kleronomos*, klay-row-**NO**-moce) denotes one who obtains a lot or portion, especially of an inheritance. If the father had only one son, there was only one heir. Christ, being God's only Son, is the heir of all things. His exaltation to the highest place in heaven marks His restoration to His rightful place (cf. **Philippians 2:6–11**).

Second, it is by or through the Son that God made the worlds (cf. **John 1:3**). Jesus is co-Creator with the Father. He was with God in the beginning, just as John also states (**John 1:2-3**). The word translated as "worlds" is *aionas* (eye-**OH**-nass) in Greek. It means, ages or times and reveals that Jesus is also co-eternal with the Father.

3 Who being the brightness of his glory, and the express image of his person, and upholding all things by the word of his power, when he had by himself purged our sins, sat down on the right hand of the Majesty on high:

Verse 3 continues the description of the Son. He is the "brightness" (Gk. *apaugasma*, ah-**POW**-gas-mah) of God's glory. The meaning of the word *apagausma* is not entirely clear. It could mean something like "radiance or splendor." If the word is understood this way, Jesus is the revelation of the brightness of God's glory. The term could also mean "reflection"; in this case, Jesus is the reflection of God's glory. In either case, God's glory is manifested in Jesus, and we see His glory as it really is. Jesus makes it possible to know God intimately. What a blessing!

Next, the Son is described as "the express image" (Gk. *charakter*, kha-rack-**TARE**) of

God's person or being. The word *charakter* refers to the stamp or imprint left by a seal on sealing wax. The imprint has the exact form of the intricately cut seal stone. Thus, Jesus is the exact image or representation of God. When you look at Jesus the Son, you see God perfectly.

Furthermore, the Son is the One "upholding all things by the word of his power." Creation is not left on its own. Jesus is the sustainer of creation—He carries it along. The Son not only was active in the event of creation (**v. 2**), but the Son also maintains an interest in creation by continuing to move it toward the accomplishment of God's plan. He does all this by the "word of his power." The "word" (Gk. *rhema*, **HRAY**-mah; not *logos*) means command.

The word translated as "purged" is the Greek word *katharismos* (kah-thah-reese-**MOCE**), which means "cleansing" or "purification." It is most often used in the New Testament of ritual cleansing (**Mark 1:44**). However, it also has ethical implications (**1 Corinthians 5:6-7**). Here, it refers to the removal of sin. The Good News is that Christ has effected a complete cleansing at Calvary. Jesus is the Redeemer.

Verse 3 ends with the exaltation of Christ. "Sat down on the right hand of the Majesty on high" shows that Christ's saving work is complete, and He is now in the place of highest honor. The writer of Hebrews will return to this powerful image of Christ sitting down, showing that Christ's sacrifice is better than the high priests' sacrifices (**Hebrews 10:11-12**).

4 Being made so much better than the angels, as he hath by inheritance obtained a more excellent name than they.

To counter the worship of angels, the writer contrasts angels with Christ. In the first century, angels were of great interest in both Jewish and Greek religious thinking. One of the most commonly held beliefs about angels was that they served as intermediaries between God and humans. Fortunately, because of who Jesus is and His sacrifice on the Cross, we have direct access to God. There is no need for anyone else to intercede between humans and God.

The author gives various reasons why Jesus is better than angels. He has "obtained a more excellent name than they." In ancient times, a name meant much more than a differentiating mark or label. Instead, a person's name was an indication of his or her character. Paul tells the Philippian church that Jesus' sacrifice on the Cross earned Him "a name which is above every name," a name that must be honored by angels, humans, and demons (**Philippians 2:9-11**).

5 For unto which of the angels said he at any time, Thou art my Son, this day have I begotten thee? And again, I will be to him a Father, and he shall be to me a Son?

Verse 5 is a combination of two Old Testament quotations: **Psalm 2:7** and **2 Samuel 7:14**. The writer views **Psalm 2** as messianic and as bestowing great dignity on Jesus as the Son with God as the Father. In the Old Testament, angels are sometimes designated as "sons of God" (cf. **Job 1:6; 2:1**). But the truth that Jesus uniquely fit the title was announced from heaven at Jesus' baptism (**Mark 1:10-11**) and preached by Paul (**Acts 13:33-34**).

The second quotation is from **2 Samuel**. Although Solomon initially used the words, the writer of Hebrews notes that the Messiah fulfills this description more completely than did Solomon. The quotation points to the Father-Son relationship as the fundamental relationship between God and Christ. No angel can claim such a relationship. By joining **Psalm 2:7** and **2 Samuel 7:14**, the writer provides strong biblical support for the claim that the position of the angels is subordinate to the status of the Son. Christ alone enjoys a unique relationship with the Father with the designation of "my Son."

SEARCH THE SCRIPTURES

QUESTION 5
Make an outline contrasting why Jesus is better than angels.

Jesus is better than the angels because: 1. God created angels; Jesus is God and He was active in creation. 2. Angels respond to God to intercede for humans; As God the Son, Jesus sits at the right hand of the Father interceding for us. 3. Angels are named by God; Jesus has a name which is above the name of angels.

QUESTION 6
When have you seen angels worshiped, and how did/would you correct this practice?

Answers will vary.

LIGHT ON THE WORD

Son vs. son
What does it mean that Jesus is the Son of God? In today's English, "son" refers to a child who is born. But the word, "Son" in reference to Jesus does not mean child or "one born out of." Jesus is neither the product nor the offspring of God the Father. Jesus is *not* a created being. Jesus *is* God (**John 1:1**).

Son of God has an entirely different meaning than saying we have a son. Jesus is "the express image" of God. Just as a stamp or imprint is exact, Jesus is the exact image of God. When we look into a mirror, we see our reflection. Jesus is the reflection or image of God, and when we see Jesus, we see God.

While Jesus is fully God, Jesus is also fully man. Jesus took on humanity—became a sinless human—and experienced hunger and pain. Because of this, Jesus knows us completely, and He understands our struggles. Jesus sits at the right hand of the Father interceding or praying for us. Jesus is the Son of God, and Jesus is the Son of Man (**Matthew 8:20**). We have an intercessor who empathizes with our feelings, so we pray in complete confidence that we are known, and we are loved.

BIBLE APPLICATION

AIM: Students will be confident of their spiritual heritage.

Believers today can marvel at the scope of God's plan—creating a people through Abraham, establishing a nation through David, and making all of humanity who are willing to be a part of both through Jesus Christ. We may not know our ancestral roots in Africa, but we claim our spiritual heritage through the Word of God. No matter our biological parentage, we stand on the legacy of our spiritual forefathers—from Abraham to Paul, to St. Augustine, to Bishop Charles Harrison Mason, to Martin Luther King, Jr., as well as to those who lead us in the present—Bishop Charles Edward Blake, Sr.

STUDENTS' RESPONSES

AIM: Students will rise above their family limitations to be all that they can be in Christ.

Jesus is the culmination of God's work of bringing salvation to the world through one family line. Jesus is God's final and definitive word for humanity. He is our perfect example of living up to this great faith heritage. He is also our perfect example of rising above the family drama to fulfill God's plan. This week, think of one family member in your natural or spiritual family who models Christ. Thank that person for helping you in your spiritual walk.

PRAYER

For the beauty of the Gospel of Matthew and the truth that those who are included in this lineage are recipients of grace, we thank You! For grafting us into the family of God through redemption and salvation, we thank You! And for giving us a future that is rooted in the plan of God and not limited to our biological family heritage, we thank You! In the Name of Jesus, we pray. Amen.

DIG A LITTLE DEEPER

We celebrate Professor Henry Louis Gates, Jr. for his historical research, writings, and television series. "In Finding Your Roots," the celebrity genealogies Professor Gates unearths have encouraged many viewers to explore their roots. Finding countries of origin on the continent of Africa, for example, provides African Americans with a sense of belonging that answers the question, "Where did I come from?" To guide you in your search, or to experience the joy of those who did, visit "Finding

Your Roots" on the PBS website.

HOW TO SAY IT

Perez. **PEA**-rez.

Zerah. **ZEE**-rah.

Hezron. **HEZ**-ron.

Amminadab. ah-**MIN**-uh-dab.

Nahshon. **NAH**-shon.

Salmon. **SAL**-mon.

Bathsheba. bath-**SHEE**-buh.

Uriah. you-**RIE**-uh.

COMMENTS / NOTES:

_____

_____

_____

_____

_____

_____

_____

_____

_____

_____

_____

_____

_____

_____

_____

_____

DAILY HOME BIBLE READINGS

MONDAY
God's Anointed Ruler of All Nations
(Psalm 2)

TUESDAY
Blessed and Chosen in Christ
(Ephesians 1:1–14)

WEDNESDAY
Christ, Head Over All People/Things
(Ephesians 1:15–23)

THURSDAY
In the Family Line of David
(Matthew 1:6–15)

FRIDAY
God Anoints Jesus King
(Hebrews 1:6–9)

SATURDAY
Jesus, Creator and Eternal Ruler
(Hebrews 1:10–14)

SUNDAY
Expectations of Jesus Before
His Birth
(Matthew 1:1–6, 16–17;
Hebrews 1:1–5)

PREPARE FOR NEXT SUNDAY

Read Matthew 1:18-25 and next week's
lesson, "Called Before Birth."

Sources:
Henry, Matthew. Matthew Henry's Commentary on the Whole Bible: Complete and Unabridged. Peabody, MA: Hendrickson, 1991.
McGee, J. Vernon. Thru the Bible. Nashville, TN: Thomas Nelson, 1983.
Mills, Watson E., et al., eds. Mercer Dictionary of the Bible. Macon, GA: Mercer University Press, 1990.
Zodhiates, Spiros. Complete Word Study of the New Testament with Greek Parallel. Iowa Falls, IA: World Bible Publishers, 1992.

LESSON 2 • DECEMBER 13, 2020

CALLED BEFORE ~~BIRTH~~

BIBLE BASIS: Matthew 1:18–25

BIBLE TRUTH: The angel announces to Joseph that Mary is bearing Jesus, the Savior of the world!

MEMORY VERSE: "Joseph, thou son of David, fear not to take unto thee Mary thy wife: for that which is conceived in her is of the Holy Ghost. And she shall bring forth a son, and thou shalt call his name JESUS: for he shall save his people from their sins" (from Matthew 1:20-21, KJV).

LESSON AIM: By the end of this lesson, we will ANALYZE the story of the angel's announcement to Joseph of Jesus' birth, REJOICE that the birth of Jesus fulfilled God's promise to be with His people, and LIVE with greater awareness of God's abiding presence.

BACKGROUND SCRIPTURES: Matthew 1:18–25—Read and incorporate the insights gained from the Background Scriptures into your study of the lesson.

TEACHER PREPARATION

MATERIALS NEEDED: Bibles (several different versions), Quarterly Commentary/Teacher Manual, Adult Quarterly, teaching resources such as charts, worksheets/handouts, paper, pens, pencils

OTHER MATERIALS NEEDED / TEACHER'S NOTES:

_____

_____

LESSON OVERVIEW

LIFE NEED FOR TODAY'S LESSON
A newborn baby inspires us to wonder about the potential of every human life. How do we understand the designs of our lives? Joseph's call to form a family with Mary suggests that God calls us to give hope to the world through our families.

BIBLE LEARNING
The angel reassures Joseph that what is happening to Mary is by God's design.

BIBLE APPLICATION
Christians acknowledge that Joseph and Mary viewed their challenges through the eyes of hope.

STUDENTS' RESPONSES
Believers celebrate the birth of Christ during this season.

LESSON SCRIPTURE

MATTHEW 1:18–25 , KJV

18 Now the birth of Jesus Christ was on this wise: When as his mother Mary was espoused to Joseph, before they came together, she was found with child of the Holy Ghost.

24

19 Then Joseph her husband, being a just man, and not willing to make her a public example, was minded to put her away privily.

20 But while he thought on these things, behold, the angel of the LORD appeared unto him in a dream, saying, Joseph, thou son of David, fear not to take unto thee Mary thy wife: for that which is conceived in her is of the Holy Ghost.

21 And she shall bring forth a son, and thou shalt call his name JESUS: for he shall save his people from their sins.

22 Now all this was done, that it might be fulfilled which was spoken of the Lord by the prophet, saying,

23 Behold, a virgin shall be with child, and shall bring forth a son, and they shall call his name Emmanuel, which being interpreted is, God with us.

24 Then Joseph being raised from sleep did as the angel of the Lord had bidden him, and took unto him his wife:

25 And knew her not till she had brought forth her firstborn son: and he called his name JESUS.

BIBLICAL DEFINITIONS

A. Angels (Matthew 1:20) *aggelos* (Gk.)—Messenger

B. Espoused (Matthew 1:18) *mnesteuo* (Gk.)—To be promised in marriage, to be betrothed

LIGHT ON THE WORD

Prophet. The biblical prophet is a speaker for God. God communicates directly with him or her, sometimes with future predictions and sometimes with commands. When God led the Israelites out of slavery, and when He gave Moses the Ten Commandments, God spoke to the prophet Moses face to face (**Exodus 33:11**). God frequently spoke to His Old Testament people through the major and minor prophets (**Isaiah** through **Malachi**). God still speaks through individuals today, but not in a way that brings novel revelation. We now have the complete Word of God—the Bible—which speaks to all people everywhere.

Angels. The Greek word *aggelos* (**ON**-gell-oce) means "messenger," and can refer to an earthly or heavenly being. Although angels have an exalted position, the Bible warns us never to worship them (**Colossians 2:18**). Angels serve many functions, but their primary purpose is to be messengers and ministers of God to humanity (**Hebrews 1:14**). Angels deliver God's specific commands (**Judges 6:11-23; 13:3-5**). Angels assist people in times of distress (**1 Kings 19:5-7**), and angels even carry out military missions (**2 Kings 19:5-7; Daniel 10:13, 21; 12:1**). Jesus indicated the existence of personal guardian angels (**Matthew 18:10**; cf. **Psalm 91:11**).

TEACHING THE BIBLE LESSON

LIFE NEED FOR TODAY'S LESSON

AIM: Students affirm the virgin birth of Jesus.

INTRODUCTION

Jesus, the Messiah

The book of **Matthew** is called the Jewish Gospel because its intended audience is Jewish. It is rooted in Old Testament prophecy related to the coming King through the lineage of King David. The first chapter of **Matthew** presents Jesus' royal family, describing His kingly line and rightful place as heir to David's throne. His legal inheritance is through Joseph, Jesus' earthly father (**Luke 3:23, 4:22**). Jesus' lineage proves that He has the right to be called the King of the Jews.

Jesus was conceived by the Holy Spirit, which gives Him the right to be called the Son of God (**Matthew 1:18-25**). He is fully God and fully human; He is the Living Word who came down from heaven, was clothed in human flesh, and dwelled among people (**John 1:1-4; Luke 1:26-35, 2:1-7**). His virgin birth fulfilled the prophetic utterances of Isaiah (**Isaiah 7:14**). The sinless and divine nature of Jesus makes Him the only Man capable of shedding His sacred blood on the Cross to become the final atonement for our sin.

BIBLE LEARNING

AIM: Students will defend the divine conception of Jesus.

I. DIVINE CONCEPTION (MATTHEW 1:18-19)

Matthew chronicles the historical background of the Messiah's birth and introduces an unexpected divine element. When Matthew says, "before they came together, she was found with child of the Holy Ghost," he presents a problem to the Jewish concept of the Messiah. For them, the Messiah was nothing more than a human being. However, Matthew sets the stage to argue that this human being is also God.

Joseph is described as a righteous man. Unlike the Pharisees, who insisted on a rigid reading of the Law's justice, Joseph

viewed his predicament that his wife-to-be was pregnant through eyes of compassion. Pregnancy before the actual wedding could have meant that Mary was unfaithful. Had Joseph applied the letter of the Law, though, Mary would have been stoned to death. Joseph was unwilling to expose her to the disgrace of public divorce or, worse, death. He, therefore, considered a quiet divorce that would satisfy the requirement of the Law and fulfill his sense of covenant righteousness.

18 Now the birth of Jesus Christ was on this wise: When as his mother Mary was espoused to Joseph, before they came together, she was found with child of the Holy Ghost.

The beginning of this verse resumes the story announced in **Matthew 1:1**. Matthew's goal here is to show the uniqueness of Jesus' birth. Mary is betrothed to Joseph. Before they are actually married and have sexual relations, Mary is pregnant by the Holy Ghost.

Matthew said Mary was "espoused" (Gk. *mnesteuo*, muh-nace-TEW-oo, "to be promised in marriage, to be betrothed") to Joseph. To be betrothed was not the same as being engaged, though it was similar. In Jesus' day, Jewish marriage consisted of three stages. First, there was the engagement, which was usually arranged (sometimes when the boy and girl were still children) by the parents or by a marriage broker. When they were old enough to marry, a formal commitment, to which the man and woman agreed, was made. It required the confirmation of two witnesses. The betrothal agreement, the requirement of witnesses, and a betrothal period indicated intention and deliberation for marrying, not a necessity to marry.

Once the couple was betrothed or espoused, they were referred to as husband and wife—note Joseph is "her husband," and Mary is "thy wife" (**vv. 19–20**). The couple was considered married, though they did not begin living together until after the wedding ceremony, which was the third stage usually a year later. Dissolving a betrothal required a divorce, not annulment, and sexual unfaithfulness during the betrothal period was considered adultery, not promiscuity, for which the penalty was death by stoning (see **Deuteronomy 22:23–24**).

Mary's pregnancy could have been disastrous. No doubt, such a scandal was not new to Matthew's original audience. However, this twist is startling when presenting the story of the Messiah's birth. Matthew states that Mary is with child as a result of the Holy Ghost. The Greek word *hagios* (**HAH**-gee-oce), translated as "holy," implies that Mary's condition resulted from something sacred, physically pure, morally blameless, religiously righteous, and ceremonially clean. In the Jewish context, this being could only be God.

19 Then Joseph her husband, being a just man, and not willing to make her a public example, was minded to put her away privily

Joseph is righteous (Gk. *dikaios*, dee-**KYE**-oce, "just"). It means that Joseph was equitable in character and practice. It implies that he was innocent and holy. Being "a just man" means that he lived by the laws of God. Jesus often criticized the Pharisees because although they kept the Mosaic Law technically, they often failed to obey its intention. Joseph, however, was not a legalistic Jew. He obeyed God's laws literally, but also, and just as importantly, spiritually.

The single Greek word translated into the phrase "make her a public example" is *paradeigmatizo* (pah-rah-dage-mah-**TEED**-zo), which means to put to open shame. When a single woman has a baby in a small town, everyone is going to know eventually. Nazareth was no different. Joseph, however, wants to avoid any public humiliation for Mary. Therefore, he decides to divorce her "privily," that is, privately and quietly. Even though he and Mary are only engaged, breaking off that engagement is as severe as a divorce. During His ministry, Jesus would use the same word for divorce that Matthew uses here, "to put her away" (Gk. *apoluo*, ah-po-**LOO**-oh) (**Matthew 5:31-32, 19:7-9**).

SEARCH THE SCRIPTURES

QUESTION 1
Why are Joseph's responses so admirable?

Joseph could have responded in a jealous rage rather than as a just and righteous man. Answers will vary.

QUESTION 2
When faced with a troubling situation, why is it right to pause and reflect before responding?

Answers will vary.

LIGHT ON THE WORD

A Just Man
Joseph decided to dissolve his engagement with Mary privately. Joseph's just nature demonstrates mercy and compassion. What made Joseph "just" was the fact that he was determined to take a different position than that of the ordinary man. Rather than submit Mary to the sanction of the Law, Joseph chose the mercy of the Law because

he was not willing to make her a public example. To "will" is to be inclined or glad to do a thing. Just people do not delight or desire to see others hurt even when they are the ones wronged. Joseph is not only an innocent man; he is also a deeply religious man. Joseph's profound reflection led him to act in ways that set him apart from his generation. What a lesson for us all!

II. DIVINE CORRECTION (vv. 20-23)

God sent an angel to speak to Joseph in a dream. This divine correction contained three vital truths. First, Joseph was reassured that Mary had not been unfaithful (**v. 20**). Joseph must see this Child as God's Child, and this event as a God-event. Second, the angel told Joseph that the baby would be a boy and that He was to be named Jesus. The name "Jesus" is a Greek form of the Hebrew name Joshua, which means "the Lord saves." Third, the angel revealed to Joseph the baby's divine purpose: "he shall save his people from their sins" (**v. 21**).

20 But while he thought on these things, behold, the angel of the LORD appeared unto him in a dream, saying, Joseph, thou son of David, fear not to take unto thee Mary thy wife: for that which is conceived in her is of the Holy Ghost.

A divine messenger brings tidings to many of God's people in times of confusion. In Joseph's confusion, he chose to be contemplative. While Joseph thought about all that was happening, God sent a heavenly messenger to lend clarity to Joseph's confusion. The words of God's messenger directed Joseph to respond correctly.

The angel addresses Joseph by name and calls him "son of David," which reminded

Joseph of his ancestry. Joseph's connection with David immediately assures him of the covenant promise given to King David regarding the coming Messiah. Since the Gospel of Matthew was addressed primarily to Christians from a Jewish background, clarity about Joseph's Davidic ancestry was essential. The angel then addresses the fact that Mary is pregnant but assures Joseph that the Child is one of divinity.

21 And she shall bring forth a son, and thou shalt call his name JESUS: for he shall save his people from their sins.

In this verse, the angel announces to Joseph that the Child is to be named Jesus. Joseph may have wondered, What is the purpose of all this? First, the angel dealt with the immediate future—the Child will be a son. Second, the Child shall be named Jesus. Jesus (Gk. *Iesous*, **YEAH**-soos) is the Greek form of Joshua (Heb. *Yehoshua*, ye-ho-**SHOO**-ah), which means "Yahweh is salvation," a reminder of the great warrior conqueror who delivered the Children of Israel from their enemies by the power of God. Finally, the angel connects the name of the Child with the Child's purpose, "he shall save his people from their sins." Jesus' name not only communicated God's spiritual purpose for Jesus, but also identified Jesus with God's purpose—to provide the means of salvation. God sent Jesus to earth, and, in obedience, Jesus fulfilled His name by dying (and rising) to save the world from sin.

Even though the modern Christian quickly thinks of eternal life in the spirit and beyond the grave as the word "save" (Gk. *sozo*, **SOAD**-zo), the use of the word here addresses the salvific view of the people of the Jews. Living amid oppression, Joseph would have understood this term about deliverance and protection. The word "save" also implies healing and preservation. In this period of Israel's oppression, salvation spoke to their need for well-being and wholeness. Many Jews wanted, and most expected, a Messiah who would set them free politically from Roman domination to once again become a mighty nation. What made Jesus unique and brought about His rejection was that God's purpose for Him was to set people free spiritually from the power and penalty of sin.

22 Now all this was done, that it might be fulfilled which was spoken of the Lord by the prophet, saying,

Matthew's deep entrenchment in Israel's prophetic tradition points us back to the Old Testament. Matthew insists throughout his Gospel that Jesus is the Messiah because He fulfills all the prophecies in astonishing ways. Matthew explains that these events have been spoken of by the prophets. Jesus' birth is the fulfillment of the divine purpose and is a long process of development, which continues within history. "That it might be fulfilled" is a common refrain throughout Matthew's Gospel (see **4:14; 8:17; 12:17**). "Fulfill" (Gk. *pleroo*, play-**ROW**-oh) means to make replete, to make completely full. This experience furnishes Joseph with an explanation of the text in the Old Testament.

23 Behold, a virgin shall be with child, and shall bring forth a son, and they shall call his name Emmanuel, which being interpreted is, God with us.

The Hebrew word Isaiah used here is *'almah* (**AL**-maw), which refers to a young female. At this stage of life, a woman would be ready for marriage or just married. In biblical times, females married at a very

early age, and the bride was expected to be a virgin. The word's meaning emphasizes the woman's youth, though she is also understood to be virginal. When the Old Testament was translated into Greek, the word used here was *parthenos* (**PAR**-theh-noce) for the equivalent stage of life, but the idea of virginity comes more to the fore. The name Emmanuel explains the nature of the child who is to be born. Emmanuel is the combination of *im* (Heb. **EEM**), which means with, a suffix meaning us (-*nu*, **NEW**), and the word *el* (Heb. **ELL**), which means God. Isaiah spoke of how God's blessings would reveal Him to be the "With-us God," but Matthew shows his audience that Jesus is the incarnate "With-us God."

SEARCH THE SCRIPTURES

QUESTION 3
Why did the angel address Joseph as "son of David"?

The angel reminded Joseph of his lineage to the Messiah.

QUESTION 4
Why is it vital that God is a "With-us God"?

Answers will vary.

LIGHT ON THE WORD

God Keeps His Word
God's revelation of His divine plan is amazing in Matthew's account of the circumstances that surround the birth of Christ. Isaiah prophesied in a message to King Ahaz about a coming birth and the salvation of God's people (**Isaiah 7:10-16**). Matthew explains that what had been promised is now being executed. Isaiah and Matthew understand the fulfillment

of this prophecy differently. At that time, Isaiah saw the Israelites and Syrians joining to fight the nation of Judah. Isaiah spoke God's words to the king: before a young woman could conceive and give birth, it would be evident that God was with His people. Before the child would learn right from wrong, the land would be even more prosperous than before (**Isaiah 7:14-17**).

Isaiah saw his prophecy come true. In less than a year (time for a maiden to marry, to conceive, bear, and name her child), Judah was indeed delivered from the army's threat. But then the Greek translation of Isaiah's words highlight a more precise understanding as Matthew reports Christ's birth. More than just a young girl having a baby, a young girl who was a virgin would have a baby. More than just feeling God's presence in His blessings on His people, God's people would genuinely experience His presence. God had already kept His word to Isaiah. With the birth of the Messiah, God keeps His word again. This time its fulfillment abundantly overflows to an extent few had imagined.

III. FROM DIVINE CLARITY TO HUMAN OBEDIENCE (vv. 24-25)

God didn't choose just any virgin or any carpenter—and there were likely scores of both in Nazareth. Instead, God chose the couple who would, individually and together, place His will above all else. Their individual and collective actions made the family that paved the way for the new community that would be known as one that fosters belonging and acceptance.

24 Then Joseph being raised from sleep did as the angel of the Lord had bidden him, and took unto him his wife: 25 And knew her not till she had

brought forth her firstborn son: and he called his name JESUS.

When Joseph wakes up from this dream, he immediately obeys its message. Joseph agrees to the solution that the angel had proposed. It also implies that Joseph is committed to acting in recognition of all that God revealed to him. What God had ordained was now going to be Joseph's purpose.

When Matthew said Joseph "took" Mary as his wife, that simple word says so much. First, it means he accepted her as his wife. Second, he abandoned any suspicion about infidelity by Mary. Third, although the Scripture gives no specifics, Joseph proceeded with the wedding and the Jewish tradition that accompanied a marriage. Fourth—and most importantly—Joseph became indispensable in preparing for the Savior's life during Mary's pregnancy.

The phrases "knew her not" and "till" mean that Joseph continued in a state of abstinence during Mary's pregnancy. After Jesus was born, Joseph and Mary would live together as husband and wife for many years. Together, Joseph and Mary had several children of their own.

SEARCH THE SCRIPTURES

QUESTION 5
Why is Joseph's obedience instructive? What do we learn?

Joseph obeyed as soon as he woke up from his dream. We learn to obey God immediately.

QUESTION 6
Is there a situation about which you need clarity? What steps might you take?

Answers will vary.

LIGHT ON THE WORD

God Speaks Today

God still speaks to us today! We may prefer the supernatural angel visitation or to hear a prophetic word from a pastor or preacher, but such experiences are not the norm. God speaks to us through His Word. If we read the Bible daily, God will provide us with the tools we need to live according to His will. God's will is God's Word, and we should obey.

Too many of us spend time questioning God when we should take a lesson from Joseph. God's commands are designed to keep us safe; God is not attempting to prevent His children from enjoying life. After God told Joseph what to do, his opinion no longer mattered. Joseph chose to please the One who was in charge of his life. Might we do the same?

BIBLE APPLICATION

AIM: Students will learn the value of silent obedience.

We never hear Joseph speak. When Joseph was disgraced and humiliated by the news of his betrothed's pregnancy, we never hear him speak. When Joseph is told to marry the woman with whom by law he should have severed ties, we never hear him speak. When Joseph learns of Herod's plot to kill Mary's baby, we never hear Joseph speak. When Joseph learns about Herod's death, we never hear him speak. When Joseph realizes that he must take his young bride and the baby Jesus to live in the despised and unimportant town of Nazareth, we never hear Joseph grumble or complain. Why? Is he not human like the rest of us? Surely he must have had strong feelings about the stress and mess of life.

Whatever his feelings may have been, Matthew portrays Joseph as one who guards his tongue. Given all the pressures that crowded in upon Joseph, why do we never hear him vent his feelings? Joseph's aim in life was obedience. The only speaking that Joseph does is through his active response to the Lord's commands.

STUDENTS' RESPONSES

AIM: Students will commit to spending time with God every day.

Divine clarification leads to the practical application of God's Word. God reveals things to us so that we might act in concert with the movement of His Spirit in the world. Insights are not given to us so that we can harbor and hoard them for self-promotion, but to create within ourselves a motion to action. God can use us to unfold this divine will, just as He did with Joseph. All we need to do is listen to the Word of God . . . and obey!

This week, reflect on the question: How committed am I to obeying God's Word? Pray and ask God to help you make decisions and govern your family life and relationships in ways that reflect obedience to His will. May your actions reflect your dedication to doing the will of God!

PRAYER

Father, thank You for sending Jesus into the world to save us from our sin. Thank You for the example of Joseph, who spent time in meditation and silence during his confusion. When we face problems in our lives, teach us to be quiet. Teach us to be silent. Teach us to meditate on Your Word, and teach us to listen to Your instructions. And, like Joseph, may we obey You without argument. Use us to fulfil your will on the earth, and may we be Your humble agents empowered by the Holy Spirit. In the Name of Jesus, we pray. Amen.

DIG A LITTLE DEEPER

Divorce. Christian marriages are not immune to the trauma of divorce. According to Christian researcher George Barna, 32% of born again Christians divorce compared to 33% of adults who are unsaved (non-born again). Barna despairs that couples do not complete pre-marital counseling before marrying. And, many couples decide to live together or cohabitate before making the marriage commitment.

On the Barna website in the article, "New Marriage and Divorce Statistics Released," Barna writes: "Government statistics and a wealth of other research data have shown that cohabitation increases the likelihood of divorce, yet cohabiting is growing in popularity. Studies showing the importance and value of preparing for marriage seem to fall on deaf ears. America has become an experimental, experience-driven culture. Rather than learn from objective information and teaching based on that information, people prefer to follow their instincts and let the chips fall where they may. Given that tendency, we can expect America to retain the highest divorce rate among all developed nations of the world."

Pre-marital counseling and abstinence are the formula for a successful marriage. He who has ears to hear, let him—and her—hear!

HOW TO SAY IT

Davidic. dah-VID-ik.

Aramite. AIR-am-ite.

DAILY HOME BIBLE READINGS

MONDAY
Sign of God's Presence
(Isaiah 7:10–15)

TUESDAY
Called a Light of the Nations
(Isaiah 42:1–9)

WEDNESDAY
Called to Mission Before Birth
(Isaiah 49:1–7)

THURSDAY
Birth of Jesus Foretold to Mary
(Luke 1:26–38)

FRIDAY
Simeon Foretells Jesus' Ministry
(Luke 2:34–38)

SATURDAY
Mary, in the Lineage of Ruth
(Ruth 4:9–17)

SUNDAY
Miracle of the Holy Spirit Conception
(Matthew 1:18–25)

PREPARE FOR NEXT SUNDAY

Read Matthew 2:7-15 and next week's lesson, "A Regal Response to Holy Light."

Sources:
Baab, O.J. "Virgin," Interpreters Dictionary of the Bible. Vol. 4. R–Z. Nashville, TN: Abingdon Press, 1962.
Barna, George. "New Marriage and Divorce Statistics Released," The Barna Group. www.barna.com
Filson, Floyd V. The Gospel According to St. Matthew. Peabody, MA: Hendrickson Publishers, 1987.
Green, Michael. Matthew for Today: Expository Study of Matthew. Dallas, TX: Word Publishing, 1988.
Hobbs, Herschel H. The Gospel of Matthew. An Exposition of the Four Gospels, Vol. 1. Grand Rapids, MI: Baker Book House, 1965.
Lightfoot, John. A Commentary on the New Testament from the Talmud and Hebraica. Matthew–1 Corinthians. Vol. 2. Matthew–Mark. Grand Rapids, MI: Baker Book House, 1979. (Reprinted from 1859 edition.)
Schweizer, Eduard. The Good News According to Matthew. Atlanta, GA: John Knox Press, 1975.

A REGAL RESPONSE TO HOLY LIGHT

BIBLE BASIS: Matthew 2:7–15

BIBLE TRUTH: The wise men honor the Child Jesus by presenting gifts to Him.

MEMORY VERSE: "And when they were come into the house, they saw the young child with Mary his mother, and fell down, and worshipped him: and when they had opened their treasures, they presented unto him gifts; gold, and frankincense and myrrh" (Matthew 2:11, KJV).

LESSON AIM: By the end of this lesson, we will AGREE that the wise men point to the universality of Jesus' mission, GRIEVE for those who suffer innocently due to the world's brokenness and sin, and JOIN with peoples of every ethnicity and culture to worship Jesus, the King of all nations.

BACKGROUND SCRIPTURES: Matthew 2:7–15—Read and incorporate the insights gained from the Background Scriptures into your study of the lesson.

TEACHER PREPARATION

MATERIALS NEEDED: Bibles (several different versions), Quarterly Commentary/Teacher Manual, Adult Quarterly, teaching resources such as charts, worksheets/handouts, paper, pens, pencils

OTHER MATERIALS NEEDED / TEACHER'S NOTES:

_____

_____

LESSON OVERVIEW

LIFE NEED FOR TODAY'S LESSON
As our world gets smaller, we are more and more exposed to people who differ from us in race, culture, and religious values. Where can we find unity in such a world? By summoning wise men from far-off lands to worship Jesus, God demonstrated that this newborn King would transcend the differences that divide us.

BIBLE LEARNING
Joseph, Mary, and the Child Jesus welcome the wise men before fleeing to Egypt.

BIBLE APPLICATION
Believers will be open to the unique perspectives of people from other cultures.

STUDENTS' RESPONSES
Believers present their lives as gifts to the King.

MATTHEW 2:7-15, KJV

7 Then Herod, when he had privily called the wise men, enquired of them diligently what time the star appeared.

8 And he sent them to Bethlehem, and said, Go and search diligently for the young child; and when ye have found

33

him, bring me word again, that I may come and worship him also.

9 When they had heard the king, they departed; and, lo, the star, which they saw in the east, went before them, till it came and stood over where the young child was.

10 When they saw the star, they rejoiced with exceeding great joy.

11 And when they were come into the house, they saw the young child with Mary his mother, and fell down, and worshipped him: and when they had opened their treasures, they presented unto him gifts; gold, and frankincense and myrrh.

12 And being warned of God in a dream that they should not return to Herod, they departed into their own country another way.

13 And when they were departed, behold, the angel of the Lord appeareth to Joseph in a dream, saying, Arise, and take the young child and his mother, and flee into Egypt, and be thou there until I bring thee word: for Herod will seek the young child to destroy him.

14 When he arose, he took the young child and his mother by night, and departed into Egypt:

15 And was there until the death of Herod: that it might be fulfilled which was spoken of the Lord by the prophet, saying, Out of Egypt have I called my son.

BIBLICAL DEFINITIONS

A. Enquired Diligently (Matthew 2:7) *akriboo* (Gk.)—To perfectly follow a law; to thoroughly understand a subject

B. Young Child (v. 11) *paidion* (Gk.)—The life stage after infancy

LIGHT ON THE WORD

Herod. The Herod featured in today's Scripture passage is known as "Herod the Great." He was a descendant of Antipater, an Edomite who converted to Judaism in the 2nd century BC. A ruthless king, Herod ordered the murder of one of his wives, mother-in-law, brother-in-law, uncle, and at least three sons. The Roman Emperor appointed and confirmed the kings in Judah, including Herod. Although the Jews did not like the king because of his friendliness with the Romans, Herod brought enough stability to Galilee and Judea that he gained some independence from Rome for the Jewish people. Herod is also remembered as a great builder; his most significant achievement was renovating the second temple in Jerusalem, which was not completed until 68 years after his death.

Magi. The words "wise men," translated Magi (singular: magus), refer to a group of men who may have studied the stars. Because the Bible says they came from the East, many scholars believe they were Babylonian or Persian astrologers. The wise men first come to Jerusalem because of a star, a unique manifestation from God to indicate a Jewish king's birth. They continue to follow the star and find Jesus. Tradition says there were three wise men, but Scripture does not give the number. The idea that there were three wise men is due to the three gifts they presented to the Christ Child—gold, frankincense, and myrrh (**v. 11**). Gold represents royalty or kingship. Frankincense, which has medicinal qualities, symbolizes deity. Myrrh, also used for medicinal purposes, is an embalming oil and represents death or suffering. These were valuable gifts.

TEACHING THE BIBLE LESSON

LIFE NEED FOR TODAY'S LESSON

AIM: Students will investigate the events surrounding the birth of Christ.

INTRODUCTION

The Wise Men

The second chapter of Matthew begins with the wise men from the East who are in search of the newborn King of the Jews. Scripture says that the wise men were all from the East. To people of New Testament days, that would probably have been Babylon or Persia, which is modern-day Iran. This area was a center of much belief in astrology.

The wise men were astrologers who saw some sort of unusual star (possibly a conjunction of planets) that indicated to them that a new king of the Jews was born. Whatever the solar configuration, it is reminiscent of the star of David, and Micah 5:2 predicts that the Messiah will be born in a section of Jerusalem known as the City of David. This is significant because God promised David that there would be a king from his lineage eternally—King Jesus.

The wise men traveled to Jerusalem, the capital, where they expected to see this Child. They almost certainly arrived in a grand caravan with many servants. Hearing that a new Jewish king has been born, Herod instantly knows this must be the Messiah. The jealous and power-hungry king asks his scholars where the Messiah was predicted to be born.

BIBLE LEARNING

AIM: Students will evaluate the motives of the wise men and Herod to see Jesus.

I. FOREIGNERS BEFORE A KING (MATTHEW 2:7–8)

The paranoid King Herod took no chances on a potential rival, even if He was just a Child. After Herod's wise men or Magi as they are also called, told him where the Messiah was to be born, Herod has a private meeting with the wise men. Herod cunningly asks them to return with news of the Messiah's whereabouts so that Herod can worship Him, too. Of course, Herod has no such intentions.

We see in this biblical account different responses to Jesus. In Herod, we see outright opposition. Even though Herod is king of the Jews, he does not rejoice at his promised Messiah's birth. He sees Jesus, instead, as a rival, one who could take control away from him. Then we see the wise men—foreigners without much biblical understanding— and yet these were the ones who set aside everything else in their lives to find Him.

7 Then Herod, when he had privily called the wise men, enquired of them diligently what time the star appeared. 8 And he sent them to Bethlehem, and said, Go and search diligently for the young child; and when ye have found him, bring me word again, that I may come and worship him also.

When he discovered where this King would be born, Herod summoned the wise men "privily," or secretly. From other usages of the word (**Matthew 1:19; Acts 16:37**), we can infer that Herod wanted to avoid a public outcry. Jerusalem is already in an uproar over the Magi's arrival (**Matthew 2:3**). Herod wanted to know the exact or specific time of the star's appearance. Why? The Magi understood that the star had risen at the time of the Child's birth. Since Herod later decides to kill the Jewish males who were two-years-old or younger, we can surmise that the Magi saw the star two years before meeting with Herod (**v. 16**).

The verb "enquired diligently" (Gk. *akriboo*, ah-kree-**BOW**-oo) is related to the adverb "diligently" (Gk. *akribos*, ah-kree-**BOCE**) in **v. 8**. It is the idea of perfectly following a law or thoroughly understanding a subject.

Instead of spending his efforts to understand the Messianic prophecy, which he knew thoroughly, Herod diligently listens to what the Magi tell him so that he can destroy the baby he perceives as a rival to his throne. The birth of the Messiah is an event the Jews have been eagerly anticipating for centuries. Now, Herod learns that the Messiah has come, and instead of joy, Herod has murderous hate. Herod wants to get rid of the Child before He could be of any physical or political threat to Herod's throne.

SEARCH THE SCRIPTURES

QUESTION 1

Why is the inclusion of foreigners in the account of Jesus' birth important?

In calling these Gentiles from far away, God showed that Christ was born to be the Savior of all people.

QUESTION 2

Since the wise men follow the stars, why is it wrong for believers today to check their horoscopes?

The Bible makes it very clear that the study of horoscopes is sin (Deuteronomy 4:19).

LIGHT ON THE WORD

The Sin of Astrology

We live in troubling times. People are seeking answers to their questions. What will happen tomorrow? Will I find a job? Will I get married? Many who are desperate for answers to life's dilemmas—including Christians—turn to occult practices rather than trusting God. Occult practices are idolatry, which the Bible says is demon worship (Leviticus 17:7).

Astrology, the I Ching, palm reading, tea leaves, tarot cards, psychics, and more are all witchcraft and sorcery. These practices are an abomination or "utterly repulsive to the Lord" (Deuteronomy 18:12, AMP).

Astrology is a sin. God says to beware! "And take heed, lest you lift your eyes to heaven, and when you see the sun, the moon, and the stars, all the host of heaven, you feel driven to worship them and serve them, which the Lord your God has given to all the peoples under the whole heaven as a heritage" (Deuteronomy 4:19, NKJV). Trusting God day by day, especially when the future seems vague and uncertain, is the mandate for believers. We demonstrate our faith, knowing God will guide and direct us, provide for, and protect us.

Never should we minimize the seriousness of the occult. During Old Testament times, practicing astrology earned the Israelites the death penalty: "If there is found among you, within any of your gates which the Lord your God gives you, a man or a woman who has been wicked in the sight of the Lord your God, in transgressing His covenant, who has gone and served other gods and worshiped them, either the sun or moon or any of the host of heaven, which I have not commanded, and it is told you, and you hear of it, then you shall inquire diligently. And if it is indeed true and certain that such an abomination has been committed in Israel, then you shall bring out to your gates that man or woman who has committed that wicked thing, and shall stone to death that man or woman with stones" (Deuteronomy 17:2–5, NKJV).

God's grace prevails today, so that death is not necessarily the sentence for the sin of astrology. However, biblical history is instructive. So, what to do? Repent, find a fireplace and burn the books (Acts 19:19). The next time someone asks your astrological sign, perhaps the response might be "My sign? The Cross!"

II. FOREIGNERS BEFORE THE KING (vv. 9-11)

After leaving Herod, the wise men continued their search. As they traveled, the star reappeared and guided them from Jerusalem to Bethlehem. By the supernatural light of that star, the wise men found the Perfect Light—Jesus!

The Magi did not listen to what King Herod told them to do. God spoke to them through a dream and told them not to return to Herod. God warned the Magi, and they obeyed His warning; they returned home a different way.

9 When they had heard the king, they departed; and, lo, the star, which they saw in the east, went before them, till it came and stood over where the young child was. 10 When

they saw the star, they rejoiced with exceeding great joy.

The wise men leave Herod for the six-mile journey south from Jerusalem to Bethlehem. Herod's instruction to "search diligently" is disrupted by the star, which now becomes a guiding star for the first time. The star's reappearance confirms the correctness of looking for the Child in Bethlehem, and it guides the wise men to the specific location. An important word is the Greek word, *proago* (pro-**AH**-go), which is translated "went before." The star is a princely messenger leading an audience into the presence of a powerful King. They were led by the light, not by their wisdom.

The sight of the star made the Magi "[rejoice] with exceeding great joy." The word "rejoice" comes from the Greek word *chairo* (**KHYE**-ro), which means "to be cheerful or well-off" (cf. Philippians 4:8). Not only does Matthew use the word chairo, but he also adds sphodra. The Greek word, *sphodra* (**SFOD**-rah) is translated in the King James Version as "exceeding." As used here, it means violently or vehemently. As if these were not enough, Matthew also adds another Greek word, *megas* (**MEH**-gass), which means "big." Translated, they were high in the spirit, or they became loud in a powerful way.

SEARCH THE SCRIPTURES

QUESTION 3
Contrast the way God spoke to the Magi with the way God spoke to Joseph.

Answer will vary.

QUESTION 4
Share about a time you had to disregard an authority figure to follow God's guidance instead.

Answers will vary.

LIGHT ON THE WORD

Why Worship?

When the wise men arrived, they immediately knelt and worshiped the holy Child. The wise men worshiped Christ before He performed any miracles, preached any sermons, or healed any sick. Their worship was based solely on who He was, not what He did. They honored Jesus with gifts worthy of His divine station (v. 11). We should all do as the wise men: find Jesus, accept Him as Lord and Savior, and worship Him!

III. THE KING IN A FOREIGN LAND (vv. 12-15)

After the wise men departed, God also warned Joseph about Herod's plan. In a dream, Joseph learned that Herod was searching for the Child with the intent of killing Him. God told Joseph to pack up and move his family to Egypt. When Herod found out that the wise men were aware of his scheme and had left the country by another route, he was furious (**v. 16**). He ordered his soldiers to go to Bethlehem and kill every male two years old and younger. This tragedy fulfilled another prophecy. The destruction caused by sinful, evil humans sets a sorrowful stage that God will soon turn to joy (**Jeremiah 31**).

Joseph follows the angel's directions and moves to Egypt, which is in Africa, returning home only when Herod was dead. Because Jesus' childhood followed this journey, Matthew notes that He fulfills yet another prophecy of coming "Out of Egypt."

12 And being warned of God in a dream that they should not return to Herod, they departed into their own country another way.

God intervened to prevent the wise men from being instruments of Herod's evil work. God speaks directly to the Magi in a dream. God tells them not to return to Herod. Going back to Herod would have been appropriate for men of honor. Herod was king, and he might have rewarded them handsomely for their work. But God gave them a strict injunction.

13 And when they were departed, behold, the angel of the Lord appeareth to Joseph in a dream, saying, Arise, and take the young child and his mother, and flee into Egypt, and be thou there until I bring thee word: for Herod will seek the young child to destroy him. 14 When he arose, he took the young child and his mother by night, and departed into Egypt:

For a second time, the angel of the Lord appears to Joseph in a dream. Joseph is just as faithful to obey God's message this time as he was the last. Joseph moves his family to a nation on the African continent—Egypt. There, Joseph waits for God's word to tell him to return to the homeland. The word "until" indicates a continued need to look and carefully listen to God's guidance (cf. v. 9). To escape undetected, they leave "by night." When Joseph woke up from the dream, he immediately obeyed that very night.

Herod wants to "destroy" (Gk. apollumi, ah-**POLL**-loo-me) Jesus. Destroy can have a variety of meanings. Throughout Luke 15, the word means "lost," but in other contexts, it has more serious connotations. The Pharisees will also want to "destroy" Jesus (Matthew 12:14), a plot that culminates in His crucifixion. Herod intends to kill Jesus. He is at odds with Christ and His mission. Christ has come to free us from such tyranny, promising that "the Son of man is come to save that which was lost [apollumi]" (Matthew 18:11).

Egyptian territory at that time was a journey of at least 200 miles from Bethlehem. God specifically tells Joseph to go there instead of going to a closer destination. Heading north to Syria was possible, but it may have been a dangerous path because it went through Jerusalem, where Herod lived. The Holy Family could have also gone west to the Mediterranean Sea and set sail as far away from Herod as they wished, but that is not what God instructed. Egypt, at this time, while out of Herod's jurisdiction, was still under Roman rule, much like Judea, except that the province reported more directly to the emperor than did Herod. By fleeing to Egypt, Jesus would fulfill prophecy foretold in Matthew (v. 15).

15 And was there until the death of Herod: that it might be fulfilled which was spoken of the Lord by the prophet, saying, Out of Egypt have I called my son.

Matthew's use of Hosea 11:1 as a messianic prophecy is a mirror of Isaiah's prophecy. The prophet Hosea was speaking to the nations of Israel and Judah before the Northern Kingdom's fall to the Assyrians. Hosea warned the Israelites of the Assyrian invasion and the Babylonian exile, which will be a sorrowful time. In Hosea 11, the prophet reminds the Israelites of their history with God. His great love brought them out of slavery in Egypt.

When Hosea wrote, "Out of Egypt have I called my son," his was not a prophetic prediction. It had already happened. In the following verse, God laments that after

He brought the Children of Israel out of Egyptian slavery, the Israelites insisted on worshiping Baal in Canaan (Hosea 11:2). Matthew is not implying that this portion of Hosea's prophesy describes the Messiah.

Instead, the comparison that God is revealing through Matthew's Gospel is that Jesus is the perfect embodiment of Israel. Just as Israel came out of Egypt, so, too, Jesus comes out of Egypt. Just as the patriarchs and Israel had to flee from the threat of death, so, too, did Jesus. Moving from place to place repeatedly, especially at a young age, is similar to being homeless. Because of this, Jesus understands the nation's sorrows. Christ fulfills Isaiah's prophecy because He is "acquainted with grief" (Isaiah 53:3), and He accomplishes the Messiah's role of being a compassionate High Priest (Hebrews 2:18).

Jesus' childhood journey mirrors Israel's cultural history. Just as there's a comparison, there's also a contrast with Hosea's prophecy. Unlike unfaithful Israel, as Hosea describes them, Jesus does not worship idols or suffer the punishment of exile. Jesus obeys God the way Israel was to obey. While Jesus' experiences mirror those of Israel, His response is not sinful, but perfect. Because He perfectly endured all these trials, Jesus Christ is worthy to be our Savior.

SEARCH THE SCRIPTURES

QUESTION 5
Why is it culturally significant that Jesus spent part of his childhood in Egypt?

Egypt is on the continent of Africa. God is inclusive of people of color who are rejected by so many. Answers will vary.

QUESTION 6
How have you noticed God's protection in your life as you followed His direction?

Answers will vary.

LIGHT ON THE WORD

Out Of Egypt

Egypt was a refuge for the Children of Israel, who prospered under Joseph's protection. When there arose a Pharaoh who did not know Joseph (Exodus 1:8), fear of Israel's prosperity converted a warm welcome into a whip of slavery. Through Moses, God delivered His people and led them to the Promised Land.

The Holy Family fled to Egypt for refuge. Egypt is on the continent of Africa. Any question that God intended to include African people in His story of salvation is put to rest by the many biblical references to our Motherland.

BIBLE APPLICATION

AIM: Students will work to destroy all barriers that create divisions among people of different races, ethnic groups, genders, economic and social classes.

Believers must affirm the "humanity", "worth", and "sacredness" of all people. We should seek to foster communication, healing, and reconciliation between all people, irrespective of race, culture, gender, and religious affiliation. How does the gospel especially resonate with poor, opressed, minority, refugee, immigrant, or foreign voices?

STUDENTS' RESPONSES

AIM: Students will examine ways to welcome various cultural traditions into their worship setting.

The Magi came to Jesus and worshiped their way, by bowing to the ground and giving gifts. Are you welcoming to other cultures' worship traditions in your church?

Jesus' family left their ancestral land and lived in another country. How would you continue to worship God and be a witness of the gospel in a foreign country? As a project, network with a local charity or immigrant population to invite immigrants to participate in a worship service at your church.

PRAYER

Father, thank You for being our refuge! Thank You for welcoming everyone into the family of God. As we remember the birth of our Savior during this season, may we be sensitive to the needs that exist in our families, churches, and communities. And may we be proactive in finding ways to welcome people from different ethnicities into our fellowship. In the Name of Jesus, we pray. Amen.

DIG A LITTLE DEEPER

Herod practiced infanticide—the killing of children and babies. Unfortunately, this practice continues today under the guise of providing abortion, which primarily targets women of color. "Why is everyone so eager to champion the right to abortion for black women when we also have a right to have better schools, jobs, and housing?" asks La Verne Tolbert, Ph.D. She is a former board member of Planned Parenthood New York City (1975-1980).

Why did Dr. Tolbert agree to serve on the board? "I had completed my undergraduate studies and was working for a magazine when asked to join the board in 1975. Although I knew little about abortion, I thought by serving on the board I could help the girls in my community. Abortion had just become legal in 1973. During my first month on the board, I learned how doctors performed abortions, and I protested. Dilation-and-evacuation tears the baby apart limb by limb. It's traumatic for both the mother and her baby!

"I was especially shocked to learn that the Department of Health required a death certificate for every abortion that was performed in New York. A death certificate? A death certificate is only needed when someone has died! Planned Parenthood was determined to overturn that requirement, and they did. Today, a death certificate is only required if the baby takes a breath before it dies . . . if the baby takes a breath . . ." Dr. Tolbert is an avid pro-life advocate. Her research on school-based clinics/health centers in inner-city public schools demonstrates that children are given abortions without parental knowledge or consent to limit the growth of the Black population. To learn more, see her book in Sources list below.

HOW TO SAY IT

Antipater. an-**TEE**-pah-tare.

Magus. **MAY**-gus.

PREPARE FOR NEXT SUNDAY

Read Matthew 3:1-12 and next week's lesson, "Called to Prepare the Way."

Sources:
Adeyemo, Tokunboh, gen. ed. *Africa Bible Commentary*. Grand Rapids, MI: Zondervan, 2006. 1110–1111.
Hoehner, Harold W. *"Herodian Dynasty." The Oxford Companion to the Bible*. Bruce M. Metzger and Michael D. Coogan, eds. New York: Oxford University Press, 1993. 280–284.
Stagg, Robert. *"Herod." Holman Illustrated Bible Dictionary*. Trent C. Butler, Chad Brand, Charles Draper, and Archie England, eds. Nashville, TN: Holman, 2003. 753–755.
Carson, Matthew. *Expositors Bible Commentary Series. Vol. 8. Zondervan*. 89.
Shaw, Ian, ed. The Oxford History of Ancient Egypt. New York: Oxford University Press.
Tolbert, La Verne. *Keeping You and Your Kids Sexually Pure: A How-To Guide for Parents, Pastors, Youth Workers and Teachers*. Xlibris, 2007. 85–94.
University of Illinois Extension. *"Frankincense and myrrh."* Illinois ACES. https://aces.illinois.edu/news/frankincense-and-myrrh. Posted November 14, 2012.

COMMENTS / NOTES:

_____

_____

DAILY HOME BIBLE READINGS

MONDAY
Midwives Frustrate Pharaoh's Decree
(Exodus 1:15–22)

TUESDAY
God Answers Solomon's Dream
(1 Kings 3:5–14)

WEDNESDAY
Insight into the Meaning of Dreams
(Daniel 1:8–17)

THURSDAY
In Christ No Divisions Allowed
(Galatians 3:25–29)

FRIDAY
Gracious Ruler to Come from Bethlehem
(Micah 5:1–5)

SATURDAY
Successful Return from Egypt
(Matthew 2:19-23)

SUNDAY
Safe in the Midst of Danger
(Matthew 2:7-15)

_____

_____

_____

_____

_____

_____

_____

_____

CALLED TO PREPARE THE WAY

BIBLE BASIS: Matthew 3:1–12

BIBLE TRUTH: John the Baptist is the voice crying in the wilderness preparing the way for Jesus Christ.

MEMORY VERSE: For this is he that was spoken of by the prophet Esaias, saying, The voice of one crying in the wilderness, Prepare ye the way of the Lord, make his paths straight" (Matthew 3:3, KJV).

LESSON AIM: By the end of this lesson, we will JUDGE the reality of sin and the necessity of repentance, IDENTIFY with John the Baptist in his call to prepare the way for Christ, and REPENT of sins and bear witness to this repentance through our deeds.

BACKGROUND SCRIPTURES: Matthew 3—Read and incorporate the insights gained from the Background Scriptures into your study of the lesson.

TEACHER PREPARATION

MATERIALS NEEDED: Bibles (several different versions), Quarterly Commentary/Teacher Manual, Adult Quarterly, teaching resources such as charts, worksheets/handouts, paper, pens, pencils

OTHER MATERIALS NEEDED / TEACHER'S NOTES:

_____

_____

LESSON OVERVIEW

LIFE NEED FOR TODAY'S LESSON
Important projects require thoughtful preparation. What endeavors demand our greatest efforts in preparation? John called for people to repent of their sins and thus be ready to welcome the soon-coming Messiah.

BIBLE LEARNING
John the Baptist breaks God's 400 years of silence.

BIBLE APPLICATION
Believers repent of their sin.

STUDENTS' RESPONSES
Believers receive the Good News of Jesus Christ.

LESSON SCRIPTURE

MATTHEW 3:1–12, KJV

1 In those days came John the Baptist, preaching in the wilderness of Judaea,

2 And saying, Repent ye: for the kingdom of heaven is at hand. **3** For this is he that was spoken of by the prophet Esaias, saying, The voice of one crying in the wilderness, Prepare ye the way of the Lord, make his paths straight.

4 And the same John had his raiment of camel's hair, and a leathern girdle about his loins; and his meat was locusts and wild honey.

5 Then went out to him Jerusalem, and all Judaea, and all the region round about Jordan,

6 And were baptized of him in Jordan, confessing their sins.

7 But when he saw many of the Pharisees and Sadducees come to his baptism, he said unto them, O generation of vipers, who hath warned you to flee from the wrath to come?

8 Bring forth therefore fruits meet for repentance:

9 And think not to say within yourselves, We have Abraham to our father: for I say unto you, that God is able of these stones to raise up children unto Abraham.

10 And now also the axe is laid unto the root of the trees: therefore every tree which bringeth not forth good fruit is hewn down, and cast into the fire.

11 I indeed baptize you with water unto repentance. but he that cometh after me is mightier than I, whose shoes I am not worthy to bear: he shall baptize you with the Holy Ghost, and with fire

12 Whose fan is in his hand, and he will throughly purge his floor, and gather his wheat into the garner; but he will burn up the chaff with unquenchable fire.

BIBLICAL DEFINITIONS

A. **Wilderness** (**Matthew 3:1**) *eremos* (Gk.)—An uninhabited, deserted place

B. **Repent** (**v. 2**) *metanoeo* (Gk.)—To have a changed mind; to think again

LIGHT ON THE WORD

John the Baptist. John was a miracle child, born to childless, elderly parents—the priest Zacharias and his wife Elisabeth (**Luke 1:5–25**). While still pregnant, Elisabeth received a visit from her cousin Mary, who also had been divinely chosen to bear a child—Jesus. The baby in Elisabeth's womb jumped for joy at Mary's voice (**Luke 1:44**).

John, the cousin of Jesus, was the prophesied forerunner of the Messiah. The public reception of John's ministry was tremendous (**Mark 1:5**). John took no credit for the response to his preaching but relegated himself to the role of messenger, rather than Savior.

Wilderness. In the Old and New Testaments, the wilderness served as a place God chose to meet with, chastise, and revive His children. The wilderness was also the place where Jesus endured a forty-day fast, encountered Satan, and overcame temptation (**Matthew 4:1–11**). We often think of the wilderness as deserts, because the wilderness the Israelites wandered before entering the Promised Land is in an arid region. The word, however, merely refers to a region with a low population, a place of solitude.

TEACHING THE BIBLE LESSON

LIFE NEED FOR TODAY'S LESSON

AIM: Students will examine how God used John the Baptist to prepare the people for Jesus.

INTRODUCTION

Four Hundred Years of Silence

After a long prophetic silence, John bursts onto the scene! This sudden appearance is a stark contrast with the silence the Israelites have been enduring because God had not sent a prophet in 400 years.

The last time God had spoken to His people was through the prophet Malachi, around 400 BC. Malachi was the very prophet to foretell the ministry of John (**Malachi 3:1; 4:5**).

There are also several years between the end of **Matthew 2** and the beginning of **Matthew 3**. Near the end of **Matthew 2**, Jesus is a young child growing up in Nazareth (see **Matthew 2:21-23**). By **Matthew 3**, John, who was born only several months before Jesus, is a grown man "preaching in the wilderness of Judaea."

John did not venture into the cities to preach; people went to the wilderness to hear him. John's ministry was a preaching and baptizing ministry that anticipated the arrival of Jesus. He urged people to confess their sins, to repent, and to acknowledge the coming Messiah who cleanses from sins and provides the Spirit who enables right living (**Matthew 3:6-12**).

John's baptism was a public affirmation that the repentant and now-baptized participants were positioned to receive God's saving grace and presence. They had repented, been cleansed, and were ready to follow the imminent Messiah.

BIBLE LEARNING

AIM: Students will evaluate the importance of John's message.

I. PREACHING THE KINGDOM (MATTHEW 3:1-4)

The people recognized John the Baptist as a prophet. God had promised to send Elijah before the coming of the Day of the Lord (**Malachi 4:5**). When John came dressed in camel's hair with a leather belt, he even appeared like Elijah (**2 Kings 1:8**). John's ministry in "the wilderness of Judaea" fulfills a prophecy of Isaiah, and again links John to Elijah, who often spent time in the wilderness (**1 Kings 17:5-7; 19:4, 15**).

1 In those days came John the Baptist, preaching in the wilderness of Judaea,

Our best understanding of the phrase "in those days" is that it refers to the time Jesus resided in Nazareth (**2:23**). Matthew ends the narrative regarding Jesus' childhood and skips several years to present the forerunner of the Messiah. John the Baptist, now a grown man, is involved in a vital preaching ministry. Since Jesus is also an adult, an entire generation has passed since Joseph took Mary and Jesus to Nazareth.

The location of John's ministry draws on the biblical tradition of end-time renewal in the wilderness (**Ezekiel 20:33-38; Hosea 2:14-23**). The word "wilderness" (Gk. *eremos*, **ER**-ray-mos) means "an uninhabited place," a place which is deserted, though not necessarily a desert. John the Baptist positions himself away from the distractions of everyday life. While traveling in the Sinai wilderness, God had first begun to reveal His will to the Israelites. While hiding in the wilderness, Elijah saw the presence of God revealed in a still, small whisper (**1 Kings 19:11-13**). Now in the Judean wilderness, John the

Baptist calls the Jews to turn to God in repentance and baptism and experience His forgiveness anew.

2 And saying, Repent ye: for the kingdom of heaven is at hand.

John's message of repentance places him within the tradition of the Old Testament prophets. Again and again, God commissioned prophets—from Moses to Malachi—to call God's chosen people to turn back to Him. Given God's anticipated judgment and redemption, responding to the call to turn one's life around and live righteously is the only sane and responsible thing to do.

Like Malachi said he would, he warns that repentant people would avoid the coming judgment. "Repent" is *metanoeo* (Gk. meh-tah-**NOE**-oh), meaning "to have a changed mind," similar to the English word, which means "to think again." This change in internal thought should naturally lead to a change in external action.

"Is at hand" translates a single Greek word (*eggizo*, eng-**EED**-zo), which means "to be close by." Even though the English translation uses a present tense "is at hand," the Greek uses the perfect tense, more literally translated "has come near." The perfect tense indicates a past event that has a continuing effect on the present. John implies that he is not just announcing the Kingdom is here, but that its presence will continue to affect our lives.

3 For this is he that was spoken of by the prophet Esaias saying, The voice of one crying in the wilderness, Prepare ye the way of the Lord, make his paths straight.

This verse describes John's prophetic function as a mouthpiece for God. John's role is referenced in **Isaiah 40:3**, which Matthew quotes to demonstrate that Christ's coming was predicted and confirmed by the Word of God. **Matthew, Mark**, and **Luke** all reference **Isaiah 40:3** to John—the one whose ministry is to prepare the way for the long-awaited Messiah.

Old Testament prophecies can be fulfilled multiple times, especially when revealed to be Messianic prophecy. God will let His people see the fulfillment of His words, and then the Messiah will unexpectedly fulfill the prophecy again to a greater degree. This verse is no different. Isaiah spoke of a rejuvenation of Jerusalem after the exile in Babylonia. The prophet spoke of the Almighty God's imminent arrival and exhorted the people to prepare a road for Him through the wilderness. God's coming would bless Jerusalem and put all other nations to shame as the Israelite state was renewed through the work of Nehemiah and Ezra.

The Gospel writers saw this prophecy coming true again with the Messiah. God was coming to Jerusalem! John the Baptist declared the way to prepare for Jesus was in their individual lives, through repentance, which was then confirmed by baptism.

4 And the same John had his raiment of camel's hair, and a leathern girdle about his loins; and his meat was locusts and wild honey.

John's description indicates that he lived roughly and simply. His "leathern girdle" was a strip of hide worn at the waist and used to hold a garment in place. There is an implied comparison here with the prophet

Elijah's clothing (**2 Kings 1:8**), again pointing to John being a type of Elijah, the prophesied forerunner of the Messiah.

John's diet of honey and locusts parallels his simple apparel. Levitical Law names locusts as the only winged insects not to be treated as unclean (**11:20-23**). "Wild honey," produced without beekeepers' assistance, is mentioned in the Old Testament as nourishment (**Judges 14:8; 1 Samuel 14:25-27; Deuteronomy 32:13**). This verse does not mean to imply that these were the only things that John ate, simply that they were the staples of his diet.

SEARCH THE SCRIPTURES

QUESTION 1
Why is repentance—having a changed mind—evident in a changed lifestyle?

With a changed mind, the one who repents turns away from sin and goes in the opposite direction. Being sorry is not the same as repentance. To repent means to stop, consider, and change the behavior.

QUESTION 2
How have places of solitude been important in your spiritual journey?

Answers will vary.

LIGHT ON THE WORD

A Powerful Message
John's ministry had two emphases. First, his powerful message called people to repentance. John was intent on preaching so that people turned from their old ways to pursue God's righteousness. Second, his ministry announced the nearness of the Kingdom of Heaven.

News of the arrival of God's Kingdom caused people to repent, and also filled them with the hope of a better life. The coming of God's Kingdom or the Day of the Lord is a time of judgment. The Jews would desire to make themselves pure so they could escape God's judgment.

Repentance and hope are today's emphasis, too. We repent or change our way of thinking, which results in a new way of living. To change our way of thinking, we study and obey God's Word, meaning we read and understand what God says, and then we put into practice what God says. Practicing or doing what God says is what it means to obey. Mental assent—merely agreeing that what God says is true—is not the same as doing what God says (**James 1:22-24**).

When God's Word renews our mind, we think differently, and when we think differently, we act differently. **Romans 12:1-2** describes this process as being transformed by the renewing of our mind. Transformation is similar to the creepy caterpillar that goes into a state of metamorphosis to emerge as a beautiful butterfly. Like that caterpillar, we become new!

II. BAPTIZING THE REPENTANT (vv. 5-6)

People responded to John's message and came from all over the Jordan Valley. When they confessed their sin, he baptized them in the Jordan River. While we cannot be certain of the source of John's practice of baptism, it is likely based on various common purification rituals of the time. It is obvious from the context that his baptism was offered as a public sign that those being baptized had received and accepted his message.

5 Then went out to him Jerusalem, and all Judaea, and all the region round about Jordan.

Matthew wants his readers to know the extent of John's influence. The imperfect tense of the Greek verb *ekporeuomai* (ek-por-**YOO**-oh-my) indicates that they were repeatedly following John over a period of time. Although Matthew does not attach a specific number to indicate how many people were attracted to John's ministry, the implication is that, in spite of some opposition, the response was huge and unusual.

The Jewish historian, Josephus, also emphasizes John's reputation and influence over the people. Besides what is given in the New Testament, the primary source for biblical scholars of information on John the Baptist comes from Josephus, who describes John's practice of baptism as purification of the body by water following the purification of the spirit by righteousness.

6 And were baptized of him in Jordan, confessing their sins.

Baptism took place in connection with the people's confessions of their sins. People confess their sins and, because John was acting as God's representative, they could be assured that through the act of baptism God accepted their confessions.

Ancient bathing practices frequently involved pouring water on someone (known as "effusion") or partial immersion. While some scholars believe that John baptized by sprinkling, other scholars believe he used immersion, since *baptizo* (Gk. bap-**TEED**-zo) means "to dip" or "immerse."

The Apostle Paul uses several metaphors to explain the theological importance of baptism, including dying and rising, walking under a cloud, and walking through the sea (**Romans 6:3–6; 1 Corinthians 10:1–2**). But these are metaphors or word pictures, and as such, they lack the specific informational elements that prove helpful in discussions of how water was used in ancient baptisms.

SEARCH THE SCRIPTURES

QUESTION 3
Why do repentance and salvation precede baptism?

Repentance is turning from sin, and salvation is receiving Jesus as Lord and Savior. Jesus saves. Baptism doesn't save. Once a person is saved, baptism follows as an identification with Christ.

QUESTION 4
Describe your baptism experience.

Answers will vary.

LIGHT ON THE WORD

Baptism
Christian baptism, anticipated in **Matthew 28:18**, develops out of John's practice of baptism. John baptized people in the Jordan River, though we do not know where along the river's 156–mile length baptism occurred. John's practice of baptism grew out of Old Testament practices involving the use of water for self-washing or washing by God (**Psalm 51:7–9; Isaiah 1:16–17; 4:2–6; Jeremiah 4:14; 33:8**). However, those rituals were concerned

with purification and sanctification for service rather than baptism, which follows salvation's cleansing of sin and guilt.

III. REBUKING THE DISHONEST (vv. 7-10)

While John's ministry was fruitful, it did not go unchallenged. Even though the Pharisees and Sadducees had their differences, they were united in their opposition to John's ministry. In return, John calls them "vipers" and questions their sincerity. The religious leaders are in danger of God's judgment, as John reveals in his metaphor about the ax and tree. Their aim is solely to escape God's punishment for sin, rather than demonstrating a commitment to abandon their evil behavior and lead righteous lives.

John the Baptist also questions their pride in their religious heritage. He reminds them that God could easily turn something as commonplace as a stone into a faithful follower. Rather than automatically conferring a holier status on the Jews, being a child of Abraham means they have a clearer revelation of how God expects them to act.

7 But when he saw many of the Pharisees and Sadducees come to his baptism, he said unto them, O generation of vipers, who hath warned you to flee from the wrath to come? 8 Bring forth therefore fruits meet for repentance:

It is doubtful that the Pharisees and Sadducees wanted to be baptized. The message of repentance was offensive to these two major Jewish parties. The Pharisees were a sect that preached strict adherence to the Law of Moses, plus stricter laws just to make sure they kept

Moses' Law. The Sadducees were generally wealthier and more politically connected. Therefore, both groups were confident they were good enough in God's eyes and had little need to repent (**Luke 18:9-14**). Possibly Jewish leaders sent emissaries to hear John, apparently not because of interest as much as to investigate and evaluate the threat his popularity posed to them (**John 1:19-22**). Matthew's careful language supports this when it says they came "to his baptism" rather than came "to be baptized."

John harshly questions the religious leaders' motives. In essence, John asked: "Since you show no signs of repentance, why are you coming to this place of baptism?" His statements in **verses 8 and 9** provide a logical challenge.

9 And think not to say within yourselves, We have Abraham to our father: for I say unto you, that God is able of these stones to raise up children unto Abraham. 10 And now also the axe is laid unto the root of the trees: therefore every tree which bringeth not forth good fruit is hewn down, and cast into the fire.

The intent of John's harsh comment is clear. The Pharisees and Sadducees cannot escape the judgment of God by hiding behind their father Abraham's religious legacy. If He chooses to do so, God can "raise up children unto Abraham" from cobblestones. As Moses reminded the Israelites in the wilderness (**Deuteronomy 7:7**), there is nothing innate about being an Israelite that attracts God to them. He could remake the entire nation of Israel in a moment just from common rocks on the ground. It is a humble and contrite heart that draws God's approval (**Psalm 34:18; 51:17**), not family heritage. After The grace of God extends beyond Jewish and family borders. Like everyone else, the Pharisees and Sadducees have a decision to make, and they must make it quickly. Yes, the Kingdom is drawing near, and so is God's judgment. Both the Kingdom and God's judgment are imminent. John uses the metaphor of an unfruitful tree to talk about the consequences of an unrepentant life. Fruit-bearing trees that bear no fruit are cut down, a message, which Jesus Himself will exactly echo in His ministry (**Matthew 7:19**). In like manner, people who were created to live for God, but who refuse to do so will ultimately encounter God's retributive justice.

SEARCH THE SCRIPTURES

QUESTION 5

John the Baptist was bold in confronting the religious leaders of his day. Why is this instructive for us today?

Answers will vary.

QUESTION 6

How can we be sure to produce "good fruit" and avoid God's punishment?

Answers will vary.

LIGHT ON THE WORD

WHAT'S ATTRACTIVE?

Despite John's rough clothing and limited diet, people were attracted to John because of the quality and content of his preaching. There is a lesson in this for today's church. We like to have beautiful worship facilities, hopefully as a sign of our honor to God rather than a show for ourselves. Ultimately, though, our beautiful buildings or fashionable dress is not what attracts people to Jesus Christ.

Christian disciples are a result of preachers whose lives are transparent and who rightly handle the Word of Truth, which means they teach correctly what the Bible says (**2 Timothy 2:15**). Preachers and teachers who live the Gospel draw men and women, boys and girls to the saving power of Jesus Christ. Our lives are an open book for all to read.

BIBLE APPLICATION

AIM: Students will accept their responsibility to help bring spiritual renewal to the world.

Given the ever-present temptation of sin and evil, the church still needs John's kind of preaching ministry. Moral standards must be set and people need to be reminded of their potential for growth in the things of God. The message of repentance, forgiveness, and the call to live right can revitalize and bring spiritual renewal. The ministry of sharing our testimony and giving witness of Jesus Christ is the call and responsibility of every believer. Like John the Baptist, we too seek to awaken in people a desire for righteousness. We are to do this in the confidence that when desire is awakened, God will grant salvation through faith in Jesus Christ and convey righteousness by the power of the Holy Spirit to all who will believe.

STUDENTS' RESPONSES

AIM: Students will desire to live right for the right reasons.

While the desire to avoid divine retribution may be a motive for right living, it is not the best motive. We should desire to live right because it is the right thing to do in response to God's love for us. It is far better to pour one's energies into bringing forth fruit suitable for repentance to glorify God, rather than to pour one's energies into merely avoiding the wrath to come.

God is concerned about right motives, as well as right behavior. Repentance that is acceptable to God results in right behavior that is sustained, not by a fear of hell, but by unconditional love for God.

This week, examine your reasons for following Christ and for doing the work of the church. Are you motivated by your love for God or by fear? If you feel any fear—whether of rejection, failure, or inadequacy—meditate instead on God's great love for you. Loving God because of His love will help change your motivation.

PRAYER

Father, thank You for the ministry of preaching and teaching. Thank You for those who challenge us to repent and be baptized, and to live right so that we are pleasing to You. Help us always to be ready to share the Gospel by letting others see the light of Your truth in our lives. And may we speak boldly about the saving power of Jesus Christ to help win the lost. In the Name of Jesus, we pray. Amen.

DIG A LITTLE DEEPER

Preachers after God's own heart are those who take the time to study. The Charles H. Mason Theological Seminary at the Interdenominational Theological Center, the official school for graduate theological education in the Church Of God In Christ, has online classes for those who want to earn a Certificate in Theology. Classes may also be available at your local church or a location in your district or jurisdiction. For more information, visit the national Church Of God In Christ's website.

HOW TO SAY IT

Malachi. **MAL**-uh-kie.

Judaea. joo-**DAY**-uh.

DAILY HOME BIBLE READINGS

MONDAY
A Voice Cries, "Comfort My People"
(Isaiah 40:1–5)

TUESDAY
John the Baptist Is the Greatest
(Matthew 11:2–15)

WEDNESDAY
The Baptist's Testimony of Faith
(John 1:19–34)

THURSDAY
Jesus, the Father's Beloved Son
(Matthew 17:1–8)

FRIDAY
In John, Elijah Has Come
(Matthew 17:9–13; Malachi 4:4–5)

SATURDAY
John Baptizes Jesus in the Jordan
(Matthew 3: 13–17)

SUNDAY
John Prepares the Way for Jesus
(Matthew 3:1–12)

PREPARE FOR NEXT SUNDAY

Read **Luke 4:14-22** and next week's lesson, "Called to Proclaim."

Sources:

Aland, Kurt, ed. Synopsis of the Four Gospels. 10th ed. Stuttgart, Ger.: German Bible Society, 1993.

Barclay, William. The Gospel of Matthew: Volume 1. Philadelphia, PN: Westminster Press, 1958. 34–54.

Blount, Brian K., et al., eds. True to Our Native Land: An African American New Testament Commentary. Minneapolis, MN: Fortress Press, 2007.

Josephus. Antiquities of the Jews. 18.5.116–119.

Nolland, John. The Gospel of Matthew: A Commentary on the Greek Text. Grand Rapids, MI: Eerdmans, 2005.

Walvoord, John F. and Roy B. Zuck, eds. The Bible Knowledge Commentary: An Exposition of the Scriptures. New Testament Edition. Wheaton, IL: Victor Books, 1983. 24–25.

COMMENTS / NOTES:

CALLED TO PROCLAIM

BIBLE BASIS: Luke 4:14-22

BIBLE TRUTH: Jesus launches His ministry with a sermon in Nazareth.

MEMORY VERSE: "The Spirit of the Lord is upon me, because he hath anointed me to preach the gospel to the poor; he hath sent me to heal the brokenhearted, to preach deliverance to the captives, and recovering of sight to the blind, to set at liberty them that are bruised, To preach the acceptable year of the Lord" (Luke 4:18-19, KJV).

LESSON AIM: By the end of this lesson, we will EVALUATE the meaning and significance of Jesus' inaugural sermon in Nazareth, SENSE the impact of Jesus' pronouncement at Nazareth, and ALIGN our faith response with Jesus' call and mission.

BACKGROUND SCRIPTURES: Luke 4— Read and incorporate the insights gained from the Background Scriptures into your study of the lesson.

TEACHER PREPARATION

MATERIALS NEEDED: Bibles (several different versions), Quarterly Commentary/Teacher Manual, Adult Quarterly, teaching resources such as charts, worksheets/handouts, paper, pens, pencils

OTHER MATERIALS NEEDED / TEACHER'S NOTES:

_____

_____

LESSON OVERVIEW

LIFE NEED FOR TODAY'S LESSON
People hear conflicting messages and proclamations all the time. What message would provide answers to life's deepest problems? The worshipers at Nazareth listened to Jesus' proclamation of justice and compassion and were amazed at His gracious words.

BIBLE LEARNING
In the synagogue, Jesus takes the scroll and reads Isaiah 48:8, 9.

BIBLE APPLICATION
Believers agree that Jesus fulfills Isaiah's prophecy.

STUDENTS' RESPONSES
Believers experience Jesus' Spirit-filled proclamation of the Gospel.

LESSON SCRIPTURE

LUKE 4:14-22, KJV

14 And Jesus returned in the power of the Spirit into Galilee: and there went out a fame of him through all the region round about.

15 And he taught in their synagogues, being glorified of all.

16 And he came to Nazareth, where he had been brought up: and, as his custom was, he went into the synagogue on the sabbath day, and stood up for to read.

17 And there was delivered unto him the book of the prophet Esaias. And when he had opened the book, he found the place where it was written,

18 The Spirit of the Lord is upon me, because he hath anointed me to preach the gospel to the poor; he hath sent me to heal the brokenhearted, to preach deliverance to the captives, and recovering of sight to the blind, to set at liberty them that are bruised,

19 To preach the acceptable year of the Lord.

20 And he closed the book, and he gave it again to the minister, and sat down. And the eyes of all them that were in the synagogue were fastened on him.

21 And he began to say unto them, This day is this scripture fulfilled in your ears.

22 And all bare him witness, and wondered at the gracious words which proceeded out of his mouth. And they said, Is not this Joseph's son?

BIBLICAL DEFINITIONS

A. **Bruised** (Luke 4:18) *thrauo* (Gk.)—Shattered or completely crushed

B. **Wondered** (v. 22) *thaumazo* (Gk.)—To admire, marvel, or have admiration as at a miracle

LIGHT ON THE WORD

Synagogue. After Solomon's Temple was destroyed and many of the Hebrews went into exile, it became necessary to develop local centers of worship and instruction in the Jewish faith. Even after their return from exile and the Jerusalem Temple was rebuilt, these local centers of worship continued. Most communities of size had at least one synagogue, and some had several. Jewish sources hold that a synagogue was to be built wherever there were ten or more Jewish men. The primary meeting was held on the Sabbath (Saturday). The usual worship service consisted of the recitation of the Shema (**Deuteronomy 6:4-9**), prayers, Scripture readings from the Law and the Prophets, a sermon, and a benediction. Often the community appointed a ruler who cared for the building and selected those who participated in the worship service. Jairus of Capernaum (**Mark 5:22**), and Crispus and Sosthenes of Corinth (**Acts 18**) were rulers at their local synagogues. On many occasions, Jesus encountered opposition and conflict in the synagogues both for His teaching (**Mark 6:1-6**) and His miracles (**Luke 4:31-37**). As opposition grew, Jesus warned His disciples of a time in the future when they, too, would be persecuted in the synagogues (**Matthew 10:17; 23:34; Mark 13:9; Luke 12:11; 21:12**).

TEACHING THE BIBLE LESSON

LIFE NEED FOR TODAY'S LESSON

AIM: Students recognize that the Holy Ghost prepared Jesus for ministry.

INTRODUCTION

Preparation

At the age of thirty, Jesus submitted Himself to baptism as a sign of obedience and to initiate His public ministry. Following His baptism, the Holy Ghost led Him into the wilderness, where He endured forty days and nights of fasting and isolation. This was a period of physical weakness but spiritual strength. Three times Satan tried to tempt Jesus, making Him offers that might appeal to His humanness. But in His divine nature, Jesus endured this period and refused the devil's temptations.

Luke 4:1 says the Spirit gave Jesus the victory over Satan in the wilderness and led Him to Galilee. There, He was able to teach in the synagogues where He was well received, gaining popularity among the people. Everyone celebrated Jesus. The accolades Jesus received in Galilee did not represent the true glory of Jesus, which was to come. Still, Jesus' ministry began and ended with His glorification.

BIBLE LEARNING

AIM: Students will be led by the Spirit.

I. RETURNING BY THE SPIRIT (LUKE 4:14–17)

The opening scene of Jesus' ministry occurs in Galilee. From a glorious reception in Galilee, Jesus' next stop was His hometown, Nazareth. The phrase "where he had been brought up" gives the impression that Jesus had not been in Nazareth for a while before this visit (Luke 4:16). Jesus had devout Jewish parents who practiced the tenets of their faith.

As was His custom, Jesus went to the synagogue every Sabbath. It was usual for Jesus to participate in worship. Anyone could be invited to read the Scripture lesson for the synagogue services. Scholars are uncertain as to how the reading from the Prophets was chosen. Perhaps the particular text was left to the discretion of the person

reading. Jesus probably chose this passage as indicated by the phrase, "he found the place where it was written" (v. 17).

14 And Jesus returned in the power of the Spirit into Galilee: and there went out a fame of him through all the region round about.

Jesus' ministry was filled with the power and leading of the Holy Spirit. We first hear of the Holy Spirit descending upon Jesus at His baptism. Next, the Spirit led Him into the wilderness to be tempted. Now, we read that He returned "in the power of the Spirit." Later in His ministry, Gospel-writers link Jesus' power of the Spirit with His authoritative teaching and His miracles. Either or both of these would certainly make the "fame of him" spread throughout the region.

Galilee was surrounded by Gentile (non-Jewish) nations that exposed the Jews to a variety of secular ideas. According to the Jewish historian Josephus, Gentiles were courageous people, and many became leaders of rebellions. Galilee was a very fertile region that was able to support the masses, probably as many as three million. God planted His Son where people would hear Him.

15 And he taught in their syna-gogues, being glorified of all.

During the exile, when the Temple had been destroyed and people lived far from their home in Israel, the Jews began meeting for worship in synagogues. A town could have a synagogue if there were at least ten adult Jewish men. Worship services on the Sabbath days had a fairly consistent routine. There were no animal sacrifices in the synagogues.

At Nazareth, Jesus went into the synagogue on the Sabbath day, a habit He had formed from childhood (**Luke 2:41–50**). He grew up in the city and in the synagogue. His was a familiar face. Of course, Jesus also was familiar with the worship rituals. Worship began with prayer followed by the reading of Scripture. It was customary for seven people to read from the Scriptures—a priest, a Levite, and five ordinary Jews. Therefore, it was not strange that Jesus is handed the Scripture to read.

Since few were able to understand the original Hebrew, the reading was followed by a translation into either Greek or Aramaic. After the Scripture reading, there was a sermon or teaching. There was no professional minister, but each synagogue had an administrator who might invite a distinguished person to speak on the Scripture, which would be followed by discussion and questions.

Jesus' authoritative messages were refreshing to the people. "Glorified" is the normal translation of the Greek word used here (*doxazo*, doke-**SOD**-zo) and usually refers to honoring God. In this context, though, it more likely has the meaning of celebrating someone or holding them with honor. The people praised Jesus and His sermons; opposition had not yet begun.

16 And he came to Nazareth, where he had been brought up: and, as his custom was, he went into the synagogue on the sabbath day, and stood up for to read.

Continuing His itinerary in the Galilee region, Jesus visits Nazareth, His hometown. Nazareth was a town in the southern part of Galilee, where Jesus spent His boyhood (**Matthew 2:23**). Nazareth was a small, but beautifully secluded village nestled in the southernmost hills of the Lebanon mountain range. Although it was near major roads, Nazareth itself was isolated from nearby traffic because of the area's hills. The isolation contributed to the fact that Nazareth was a less vital part of the national and religious life of Israel. Coupled with its seclusion, Nazareth had a poor reputation both morally and religiously. Nazarenes may have spoken a crude dialect. All this seems to make Nazareth notorious, which probably prompted Nathanael, when he first learned of Jesus of Nazareth, to ask, "Can anything good come from Nazareth?" (**John 1:46, NLT**).

17 And there was delivered unto him the book of the prophet Esaias. And when he had opened the book, he found the place where it was written,

Jesus is handed the book of the prophet Isaiah (KJV: Esaias). Even though the word "book" (Gk. *biblion*, bee-**BLEE**-on) is used, we should not imagine a codex with stacked pages bound in a spine, like modern books. The Hebrew Scriptures were written on parchment, as were most writings until the 4th century AD. The prophetic books in the Hebrew scrolls were in single volumes (except the twelve minor prophets, which were written collectively on one scroll). **Isaiah** is the longest of the prophetic books, and the parchment could have been almost two feet thick when rolled up. Jesus unrolls the scroll to the prophetic passage, which summarizes His earthly mission.

SEARCH THE SCRIPTURES

QUESTION 1

Jesus' ministry was initiated after sacrifice and obedience. What lessons might this pattern teach us?

Answers will vary.

QUESTION 2

Why is it important that parents accompany their children to church just as Jesus' earthly parents did?

Answers will vary.

LIGHT ON THE WORD

A Wise Ministry Launch

Jesus has been baptized (**Luke 3:21**) and led into the wilderness by the Spirit where the devil tempted Him for forty days (**4:1-13**). Having overcome all the temptations of the devil and being filled with the power of the Holy Spirit, Jesus returns to the region of Galilee, where He officially begins His ministry (cf. **Matthew 4:12; Mark 1:14**). He is now about thirty years old (**Luke 3:23**). According to Jewish Law, this is the age priests begin their duties (**Numbers 4:23; 1 Chronicles 23:3**). From the context, Jesus has been teaching in other cities in this region (e.g., Capernaum; see **Luke 4:23**), especially in their synagogues, before reading Isaiah in His hometown's synagogue. His fame has spread all over because of the miracles and the authority with which He taught (**Luke 4:14-15; Mark 1:21-28; 3:32ff**).

II. THE SPIRIT IS UPON ME (vv.18–19)

The reading from **Isaiah** points to the very nature of Jesus' ministry. His purpose was to bring the Good News to the poor, brokenhearted, captives, blind, and oppressed (bruised). The Gospel is the Good News to those whose hope is in Almighty God to act on their behalf. Jesus identifies Himself with the social, religious, and economic outcasts of His day.

Throughout the Old Testament, God is clearly on the side of the poor and oppressed (**Isaiah 58:6; Psalms 103:6; 146:7; 72:12-14**). "The acceptable year of the Lord" (**Luke 4:19**) to which Jesus refers was likely the Jubilee Year described in **Leviticus 25**. The Year of Jubilee was a time when the economic and social inequities accumulated through the years were dismissed; God's people now had a new beginning. In Jubilee, slaves were set free! Debts were canceled! Those who were in servitude because they couldn't pay their bills were now debt-free; their ancestral lands were restored, and they were free to return to their families.

18 The Spirit of the Lord is upon me, because he hath anointed me to preach the gospel to the poor; he hath sent me to heal the broken-hearted, to preach deliverance to the captives, and recovering of sight to the blind, to set at liberty them that are bruised. 19 To preach the acceptable year of the Lord.

Jesus reads from **Isaiah 61:1-2** and includes a single phrase from **58:6**. He probably read in Hebrew and translated into Aramaic, the commonly spoken language at the time. Jesus reads, "The Spirit of the Lord is upon me," which means that He is filled with the power of the Holy Spirit. In **verse 21**, Jesus identifies Himself as the subject of Isaiah's prophecy. Now, Jesus says that the Holy Spirit has set Jesus apart for a specific ministry.

Jesus has been "anointed." The word "anointed" is translated as the Greek word *chrio* (**KHREE-oh**), which means to consecrate, ordain, or set apart a person for a particular service. It is the same word from which we get "Christ," the Anointed One. The "Gospel" did not originate in the New Testament but had its beginning in Old Testament prophetic literature. The Old Testament prophets prophesied that God would usher in a new era of justice, righteousness, and peace. During a time of great wickedness, injustice, and oppression, the prophet wrote, "Let judgment run down as waters, and righteousness as a mighty stream" (**Amos 5:24**). Jesus understood His mission as the fulfillment of this Old Testament promise. When Jesus gave His inaugural address in the synagogue, which spoke of preaching the Good News to the poor and afflicted, binding up the brokenhearted, proclaiming liberty to the captives, and opening the prison to those who are bound, it was a reminder of the familiar prophecies.

Jesus declares that He has been consecrated, as evidenced by the power of the Holy Spirit for a twofold ministry—to preach and to heal. He is called "to preach the gospel" (Gk. *euaggelizo*, yew-ang-gell-**EED**-zo), that is, to announce good news, or glad tidings, to the "poor," which includes the physically and spiritually poor. Jesus is called to preach "deliverance to the captives," those who were bound and imprisoned in sin, sickness, and death (**Acts 10:38; Ephesians 4:8-10; Hebrews 2:14-15**). He is also sent "to preach [proclaim to all] the acceptable year of the Lord," a day salvation. However, it is also a time of vengeance for the Lord. It is speaking of the end times.

The second function of the anointing is for healing, both spiritually and physically. Jesus is sent "to heal the brokenhearted." He will bring comfort and hope to the destitute in heart. The anointing is also for the "recovering of sight to the blind"— body, spirit, and soul—for those in darkness (**Matthew 4:16; Acts 26:18**). Jesus healed many people who were physically blind, but Jesus also spoke of spiritual blindness (**John 9**). Jesus is also sent to liberate those "that are bruised" (Gk. *thrauo*, **THROU**-oh, shattered or crushed, broken into many pieces), which speaks of the oppressed (**Isaiah 58:6-14**). Although Isaiah writes of Israel's captivity, the reality is to be fulfilled in the future by Christ's ministry.

SEARCH THE SCRIPTURES

QUESTION 3
Why is the Holy Ghost essential for ministry?

Answers will vary.

QUESTION 4
Have you received the gift of the Holy Ghost?

Answers will vary.

LIGHT ON THE WORD

The Anointing
In the Old Testament, people or things were anointed, as symbolized by the pouring of oil to signify holiness and separation unto God—like the tabernacle and its furniture (**Exodus 30:22ff**), priests (**Exodus 28:41**), kings (**Judges 9:8; 2 Samuel 2:4; 1 Kings 1:34**), and prophets (**1 Kings 19:16**). The anointing also symbolized authority, appointment, and equipping for a particular function or service to God. It was usually associated with the outpouring of the Spirit of God (**1 Samuel 10:1, 9; 16:13**). The anointing was always regarded as an act of God, and it meant the bestowal of divine favor (**Psalm 23:5; 92:10**). The same idea continues in the New Testament (**Acts 10:38; 1 John 2:20, 27**) and generally

refers to the anointing of the Holy Spirit. Jesus promised His disciples that they would receive the Holy Spirit.

III. SCRIPTURE FULFILLED (vv.20-22)

After His reading, the congregation was still. All eyes were fastened on Jesus, as they waited for this young rabbi to offer a sermon on the prophetic text. Jesus interrupted the silence with a profound declaration, "This day is this scripture fulfilled in your ears" (v. 21). The Messiah of God's promise was present, right in their midst. The acceptable year of the Lord is launched in the person and ministry of Jesus. He ushers in a new age of salvation. The Good News of the Kingdom is indeed the fulfillment of the Old Testament Messianic hope.

Initially, those who heard His words responded favorably even though they were confused about His identity. After all, He was Joseph's son, wasn't He? How could a carpenter's son declare Himself to be the Son of God?

20 And he closed the book, and he gave it again to the minister, and sat down. And the eyes of all them that were in the synagogue were fastened on him. 21 And he began to say unto them, This day is this scripture fulfilled in your ears.

Luke now resumes his narrative. After reading the lesson for the day, Jesus handed the scroll to the minister and sat down. Sitting was the usual position for those giving a sermon in the synagogue. As Jesus sat down, the people in the synagogue focused their attention on Him. Jesus explained to them the Scripture. We do not have the full content of Jesus' teaching. "And he began to say" suggests more was said than is recorded. Luke includes the summary of Christ's words: "This day is this scripture fulfilled in your ears."

Jesus declares that the words He has read have finally been fulfilled in their presence. In essence He says that He, Jesus, is the One anointed by God, endued with the Holy Spirit and spoken of in the Old Testament to proclaim the Good News of salvation and deliverance. Jesus will fulfill the prophecies of the Suffering Servant (**Isaiah 42:1-4; 49:1-6; 50:4-7; 52:13-53:12**), as He publicly claimed to be the Messiah.

22 And all bare him witness, and wondered at the gracious words which proceeded out of his mouth. And they said, Is not this Joseph's son?

At first, the people's reaction was that of wonder and excitement. Everyone "wondered" (Gk. *thaumazo*, thou-**MOD**-zoh), which means to admire, marvel, or to have admiration. Jesus spoke with such grace and authority that the people marveled as they would at a miracle. Jesus' words and His claim were so startling and amazing that they began to ask each other, "Is not this Joseph's son?"

Although they had known Jesus, they had never heard such words in the 30 years He had lived among them. Jesus' was the son of Joseph, an ordinary person. How could Jesus make such a claim?

This was the turning point—the religious leaders' attitude of awe and wonder switch to doubt and skepticism. Although they are simply amazed and incredulous now, some would soon be filled with indignation and anger at Jesus' words. As Jesus finishes this sermon, the people of Nazareth are so furious that they drag Him to a hill to throw Him down a cliff. But Jesus passes through the crowd and leaves (**vv. 28-30**).

SEARCH THE SCRIPTURES

QUESTION 5

Why did the people ask about Joseph, Jesus' earthly father?

They must have thought, "How can Jesus, whose father Joseph is ordinary, be the anointed One?" Answers will vary.

QUESTION 6

What stands out to you the most about this account? Why?

Answers will vary.

LIGHT ON THE WORD

Public Reading

The reading of Scripture formed an integral part of synagogue worship. Indeed, Scripture reading remains the most important part of worship in the Jewish religion even today. Before and during Jesus' time, the Jewish people read the Scripture systematically. Readings from the Law and the Prophets followed a schedule of 155 specific lessons, which allowed completion of the entire Pentateuch in three years. In both Palestine and Babylon, readings were from the Hebrew text followed by an Aramaic translation, the familiar language of the Middle East.

BIBLE APPLICATION

AIM: Students will read the Scriptures aloud.

Public reading in our churches today is limited to the Scripture reading at the beginning of service. The pastor/teacher/ speaker may also read a small portion of the Scripture that references the sermon or lesson. However, perhaps we might consider a more extensive public reading of Scripture. Unfortunately, many do not read the Bible once they leave a church service, so they don't have an opportunity to "hear" what God is saying. Today, Scripture reading and memorization are lost arts. Might we dedicate more time to publicly reading the Bible in our services and classrooms? What would happen if we sang less and read more?

STUDENTS' RESPONSES

AIM: Students will research the Year of Jubilee.

Isaiah refers to Jubilee in the context of a restoration of Israel. This week, use your Bible and Bible reference tools to research the year of Jubilee (**Leviticus 25:8–55**). Spend time meditating on how the deliverance Jesus brings compares and contrasts with the freedom of the Jubilee year. Share your thoughts with the group next week.

PRAYER

Father, thank You for loving us so much that You sent Your Son into the world to heal and deliver us, to open our spiritually blind eyes, and set us free! May we also be committed through the power of the Holy Ghost to preaching the Good News of Jesus Christ to the poor, sharing God's deliverance to prisoners, teaching the spiritually blind, and partnering with You in setting the oppressed free. In the Name of Jesus, we pray. Amen.

DIG A LITTLE DEEPER

Jesus Christ inaugurated the reign of God's Kingdom in His life and ministry. Termed "inaugurated eschatology," the blessings—and the work—began with Jesus' ministry and will be consummated at the Second Coming. While there are spiritual interpretations of poverty, blindness, and oppression, there is also the physical reality. Many people in the world worry about when they will eat their next meal—or if they will eat today at all—or worry about where they will sleep tonight, or if they can pay rent this month.

How can we help when so many are too occupied with these worries to think about spiritual matters? As Christ's hands and feet, Christians must work to meet physical needs and fight systems of oppression with justice while preaching, teaching, testifying, and living the Gospel to fill the spiritual void in people's lives (Acts 1:8).

Jesus inaugurated this work and showed us how to do it by His ministry. And Jesus has anointed us with the Holy Spirit to continue His work until the moment we meet Him in the clouds.

HOW TO SAY IT

Shema. shuh-**MAH**.

Jairus. **JIE**-russ.

PREPARE FOR NEXT SUNDAY

Read **Luke 5:1-11** and next week's lesson, "Called to Significance."

Sources:
Holman Bible Dictionary. Trent Butler, general editor. Nashville, TN: Broadman & Holman Publishers, 1991. 1311- 1312.
Josephus. The Life of Flavius Josephus.
Mishel, Lawrence, Josh Bivens, Elise Gould, and Heidi Shierholz. "Poverty." State of Working America Key Numbers. Economic Policy Institute. Ithaca, NY: Cornell University Press, 2012.

COMMENTS / NOTES:

DAILY HOME BIBLE READINGS

MONDAY
Live By God's Word
(Deuteronomy 8:1–11)

TUESDAY
Jubilee, Year of God's Favor
(Leviticus 25:8–17)

WEDNESDAY
Miracle of the Meal and Oil
(1 Kings 17:8–16)

THURSDAY
Naaman's Leprosy
Healed in Jordan River
(2 Kings 5:1–14)

FRIDAY
Jesus Overcomes
the Devil's Temptations
(Luke 4:1–13)

SATURDAY
Jesus Driven out of Nazareth
(Luke 4:23–30)

SUNDAY
Jesus' Mandate for Ministry
Announced
(Luke 4:14–22)

CALLED TO SIGNIFICANCE

BIBLE BASIS: Luke 5:1-11

BIBLE TRUTH: Jesus calls fishermen to become His disciples and fish for men.

MEMORY VERSE: "Jesus said unto Simon, Fear not; from henceforth thou shalt catch men" (Luke 5:10, KJV).

LESSON AIM: By the end of this lesson, we will EVALUATE the significance in the miraculous catch of fish, REFLECT on Simon's changing attitude toward Jesus, and RECONSIDER Jesus' instructions for us today.

BACKGROUND SCRIPTURES: Luke 5:1-11—Read and incorporate the insights gained from the Background Scriptures into your study of the lesson.

TEACHER PREPARATION

MATERIALS NEEDED: Bibles (several different versions), Quarterly Commentary/Teacher Manual, Adult Quarterly, teaching resources such as charts, worksheets/handouts, paper, pens, pencils

OTHER MATERIALS NEEDED / TEACHER'S NOTES:

_____

_____

LESSON OVERVIEW

LIFE NEED FOR TODAY'S LESSON
People seek significance and purpose. Are we on earth just to eke out a living, or can we be part of something greater? Jesus called Simon and his cohorts to follow Him and find fulfillment in doing the work of God's kingdom.

BIBLE LEARNING
Simon Peter and the disciples were ordinary men whose lives were changed by an extraordinary Teacher.

BIBLE APPLICATION
Believers will respond to the call to be Jesus' disciples.

STUDENTS' RESPONSES
Spiritually mature believers will disciple others.

LESSON SCRIPTURE

LUKE 5:1-11, KJV

1 And it came to pass, that, as the people pressed upon him to hear the word of God, he stood by the lake of Gennesaret,

2 And saw two ships standing by the lake: but the fishermen were gone out of them, and were washing their nets.

3 And he entered into one of the ships, which was Simon's, and prayed him that he would thrust out a little from the land. And he sat down, and taught the people out of the ship.

4 Now when he had left speaking, he said unto Simon, Launch out into the deep, and let down your nets for a draught.

5 And Simon answering said unto him, Master, we have toiled all the night, and have taken nothing: nevertheless at thy word I will let down the net.

6 And when they had this done, they inclosed a great multitude of fishes: and their net brake.

7 And they beckoned unto their partners, which were in the other ship, that they should come and help them. And they came, and filled both the ships, so that they began to sink.

8 When Simon saw it, he fell down at Jesus' knees, saying, Depart from me; for I am a sinful man, O Lord.

9 For he was astonished, and all that were with him, at the draught of the fishes which they had taken:

10 And so was also James, and John, the sons of Zebedee, which were partners with Simon. And Jesus said unto Simon, Fear not; from henceforth thou shalt catch men.

11 And when they had brought their ships to land, they forsook all, and followed him.

BIBLICAL DEFINITIONS

A. Master (**Luke 5:5**) *epistates* (Gk.)— Teacher, emphasizing the teacher's position of respect

B. Beckoned (**v. 7**) *kataneuo* (Gk.)—To signal by nodding one's head

LIGHT ON THE WORD

Lake Gennesaret. The Lake of Gennesaret is also known as the Sea of Galilee. It is called Gennesaret because the fertile Plain of Gennesaret lies on the northwest side of the lake (**Matthew 14:34**). The Old Testament calls it the Sea of Chinnereth because of the shape of it (Hebrew "harp-shaped," **Numbers 34:11**) and "Chinneroth" (**Joshua 12:3**) from the town so named on its shore. Gennesaret is probably the corruption of the name Chinneroth. The Sea of Tiberias is another designation (**John 6:1; 21:1**), associated with the capital of Herod Antipas. All of the names of this single body of water were derived from places on the western shore. The lake is some 60 miles north of Jerusalem.

Sea of Galilee. The Sea of Galilee was the focus of Galilee's wealth. Nine cities with a population of 15,000 or more stood on its shores. To the northwest was Capernaum, the home of Simon and Andrew (**Mark 1:29**), and it is here that Matthew sat at custom (**Matthew 9:9**). The Sea of Galilee measures 13 miles north to south and 7 miles east to west and encompasses much of Jesus' Galilean ministry.

TEACHING THE BIBLE LESSON

LIFE NEED FOR TODAY'S LESSON

AIM: Students will obey Jesus' call.

INTRODUCTION

Go!

Previously in **Luke**, the Lord Jesus was in Capernaum (**Luke 4:31**), healing many people who came to Him (**vv. 40-41**). After these many mighty works, Jesus slipped away to pray in a deserted place near the city. His disciples found Him and reported that many people wanted Jesus to remain with them. But Jesus told them that He had to go to the other cities and preach the Kingdom of God, for that is what He was sent to do (**v. 43**).

His mission was not to call others from a single place but to go to people throughout Judea—where they worked, where they lived, where they studied—and minister to them where they were. Jesus left Capernaum to preach in other cities of the Decapolis (see **Matthew 4:25**). His first stop was Lake Gennesaret (i.e., the Sea of Galilee), where He makes contact with a crowd of people and with some of the men whom He would call to be His disciples.

BIBLE LEARNING

AIM: Students will stretch the boundaries of their ministries.

I. THE MULTITUDE (LUKE 5:1-3)

One morning, Jesus was on the shore of Lake Gennesaret, near Capernaum. As a result of His fame, a great multitude had already gathered to listen to His teaching. The Lord sat down in Simon's ship—one of two that were standing by the shore of the lake—so that the crowds could hear Him. Then, Jesus asked Simon to push the boat out a little further from land, and from there Jesus taught the multitude.

1 And it came to pass, that, as the people pressed upon him to hear the word of God, he stood by the lake of Gennesaret.

This event took place on the shore of the Sea of Galilee, a body of water that has many names. This is the only verse where the lake is called by the Greek name of the town that was located on the northwest shore of the lake, Gennesaret. Usually, the Gospel writers refer to the lake with the name of the larger Jewish district to the west of the lake, Galilee. Luke uses the word "lake," but the other evangelists follow the pattern of the Old Testament and call it a sea.

After Jesus' baptism and temptation in the wilderness, He began His ministry in Galilee. He became known all over Galilee (**4:14**). His preaching ministry affirmed with the signs and wonders, attracted the crowds (**4:42**). The people wanted to listen to the word from God and were eager for a revelation about God. They were "amazed" by the grace and authority of His words (**4:22, 32**) and gathered to see Him by the shore of the Sea of Galilee.

2 And saw two ships standing by the lake: but the fishermen were gone out of them, and were washing their nets.

After each day of fishing, the equipment was cleaned and repaired for the next expedition. Fishermen pulled their boats out of the water or into the shallow water close to land to prevent them from drifting away. Fishing boats usually worked in pairs, dragging a net between them. An average fishing boat would be about twenty to thirty feet long. These two boats were empty because the fishers didn't catch any fish during their day's work.

3 And he entered into one of the ships, which was Simon's, and prayed him that he would thrust out a little from the land. And he sat down, and taught the people out of the ship.

Jesus chose one of the boats and asked its owner, Simon, to push the boat into the water. Simon does as Jesus requested. The crowds could hear Jesus perhaps because the shape of the sea echoed His voice.

SEARCH THE SCRIPTURES

QUESTION 1
Why were the multitude so eager to hear Jesus teach?

The people wanted to hear a revelation about God. They were amazed by His grace and authority. Answers will vary.

QUESTION 2
Why does Jesus choose fishermen to help Him in His ministry?

Answers will vary.

LIGHT ON THE WORD
Creative Spaces
Jesus taught in creative spaces. On this occasion, Jesus stepped into a boat rather than teaching inside a synagogue. Jesus taught where the people gathered. The Bible tells us to "Go ye into all the world" (from **Mark 16:15**). The Bible does not tell the world to come to us. Wherever the opportunity, believers should be ready and committed to go and share the Good News of Jesus Christ!

II. THE MIRACLE (vv. 4-7)
After He finished teaching, Jesus commanded Simon to launch out from the shore into the deeper part of the lake (**v. 4**). Simon protests. They had fished all night, which was the best time for fishing, and had already washed their nets. Nevertheless, at Jesus' words, they obeyed His command.

Jesus rewards their faith! They catch so many fish in their nets that they have to call their partners in another boat to come and help. Both boats become so full of fish that they cannot hold the catch.

4 Now when he had left speaking, he said unto Simon, Launch out into the deep, and let down your nets for a draught.

Jesus addresses Simon as the captain of the boat to take Simon's fishing team out with him to put down the nets, which required two to four men to deploy. The Greek word used for net is *diktuon* (**DEEK**-too-on). Jesus' use of the word "draught" (American spelling: draft) refers to things that are drawn or pulled, implying these are a type of dragnet. These nets were made of linen, which would be visible to fish during the day. Colder water can hold more oxygen for the fish to breathe, so they will be more active when the water of the lake is cooler, as at nighttime. That is why Simon's crew fished at night. To be able to catch fish in broad daylight was a miracle.

5 And Simon answering said unto him, Master, we have toiled all the night, and have taken nothing: nevertheless at thy word I will let down the net.

Simon demonstrates respect. Although Simon is a professional fisherman, he does not despise the instruction of Jesus. Simon was probably brought up in this trade, since children usually inherited their parents' profession. After an exhausting night's work, Simon could convincingly state that there was no need to try again.

The Greek word used for "master" is *epistates* (eh-peese-TAH-tace). In the New Testament, the word only appears in **Luke** and is used when addressing Jesus, replacing the title of rabbi and teacher, which are used in the other Gospels. The word, master, still means "teacher" and is used to address a person of high status or a person in a leadership role.

6 And when they had this done, they inclosed a great multitude of fishes: and their net brake. 7 And they beckoned unto their partners, which were in the other ship, that they should come and help them. And they came, and filled both the ships, so that they began to sink.

What a contrast from the beginning of the passage! The two empty boats were now full of fish and about to sink. Obeying Jesus' command resulted in the unexpected. The Greek word used for "beckoned" is *kataneuo* (ka-ta-NEW-oh). It means "to signal by nodding one's head," suggesting that Simon's company could not wave to their partners in other boats. Their hands were busy pulling the nets out of the water; their partners from the other ships responded to Simon's nod.

SEARCH THE SCRIPTURES

QUESTION 3

Why is Simon's obedience to go fishing again a demonstration of his faith?

Obedience—without seeing or understanding the outcome—is an act of faith. Answers will vary.

QUESTION 4

When have you had "nevertheless" faith?

Answers will vary.

LIGHT ON THE WORD

Nevertheless

We need "nevertheless" kind of faith in our lives today. "Nevertheless" faith means that, no matter what the obstacles are, we are going to obey God's Word—the Bible. Obedience equals faith. Disobedience equals lack of faith. It doesn't get any more simple than that!

III. THE NEW MINISTRY (vv. 8-11)

The Lord's power makes a powerful impression on Simon. He falls before the Savior, overwhelmed by His divine glory and with a deep realization of his own utter sinfulness. Jesus understands Simon's state of mind and speaks to him reassuringly. Simon receives a divine calling to evangelism, and Simon, James, and John commit to follow Jesus. They have no idea what they were going to be involved in, only that they would "catch men" (**v. 10**). Still, they dropped their nets, which means they left their vocation and followed Jesus.

8 When Simon saw it, he fell down at Jesus' knees, saying, Depart from me; for I am a sinful man, O Lord.

Simon has never witnessed such a thing before. He becomes suddenly aware that this Man is divine. Earlier, Simon used the title "master" for Jesus (**v. 5**), but now he calls Him "Lord" (Gk. *kurios*, **KOU**-ree-oce). The word is a polite title, and it is also used to address God. Simon is aware that the Person with whom he is dealing is no ordinary man.

Simon, overwhelmed with his unworthiness, admits he is a sinful man and asks Jesus to leave him. Simon correctly assesses the condition of his heart and the glory of Christ, but his reaction is not salvific. Instead of wanting to be cleansed and united with God's glory so that he may enjoy God's presence, Simon cowers in fear. Simon's focus on himself implies selfishness rather than self-reflection.

9 For he was astonished, and all that were with him, at the draught of the fishes which they had taken: 10 And so was also James, and John, the sons of Zebedee, which were partners with Simon. And Jesus said unto Simon, Fear not; from henceforth thou shalt catch men.

The magnitude of the catch is not only to Simon's amazement, but also to the amazement of his partners. Jesus calms Simon's fear and changes the destiny of Simon's life. From now on, Simon and his fishing crew will be fishers of men. Jesus' commission of Simon, who readily admits he is a sinner, lays the groundwork for Jesus' ministry of forgiveness and the growing reputation of Jesus as a friend of sinners.

11 And when they had brought their ships to land, they forsook all, and followed him.

When they reach dry land, Simon, James, and John decide to leave everything to follow Jesus. These men are so convinced that Jesus will meet all their needs that they were willing to entrust themselves to His providential care. In Jesus, the new disciples have found a more fulfilling life than fishing.

SEARCH THE SCRIPTURES

QUESTION 5
Why did Jesus use the analogy that Simon will now be a fisher of men?

As a fisherman, Simon could relate to this analogy or word picture. He knew how to catch fish. Now he is beginning to understand that he has a new role—"catching" men to follow Jesus.

QUESTION 6
As a disciple, have you left all to follow Jesus? Why? Why not?

Answers will vary.

LIGHT ON THE WORD
Leaving All
When we meet Jesus, we too, must confess that we are sinful and need to be made whole. We should be willing to forsake all and follow Jesus. Jesus is looking for those with humble hearts to boldly respond to His call by faith. This experience is a turning point for Simon and his colleagues. They will have a changed mindset and a new vocation. Simon exhibits a willingness to learn. He knows he is lacking and sinful, but Simon obeys the Master's voice to see what God can do. May we be as obedient!

Jesus called men from their vocation of fishing to a labor of a different sort. When these humble disciples become "fishers of men," they develop into powerful witnesses who turn the world upside down.

BIBLE APPLICATION

AIM: Students will evaluate their skills and talents for ministry.

The disciples switch their focus from fishing for fish to fishing for people. They will need some of the same skills for ministry that they used in their vocation. What natural talents do you use in your profession that you can use to spread the Gospel?

While the fishermen left their nets to follow Jesus, the men also had a network of support that freed them to focus on full-time ministry. How can your Bible study group or church lend background support so others are financially able to devote themselves to the ministry?

STUDENTS' RESPONSES

AIM: Students will recommit to being Jesus' disciples.

Think about the commitment you've made to Jesus. Are you still excited about it? If not, ask God to revive you so you can become a fisher of men. Encourage one another!

PRAYER

Father, we will follow Jesus! Please use our gifts and talents and channel them into the work of the Kingdom. In the Name of Jesus, we pray. Amen.

DIG A LITTLE DEEPER

All Jewish boys learned the Torah. Students who showed promise were invited to keep studying the Prophets and then were asked to study of the poetic Writings of the Hebrew Bible. To these students, a rabbi would simply say, "Follow me."

Students would never turn down the great honor of studying under a rabbi. Those who did not seem bright enough to keep studying returned home to learn the family trade.

Simon and his companions were engaged in their family trade the day Jesus called them to follow Him. At some point in their education, they may not have been considered gifted enough to continue studying.

Perhaps no rabbi wanted them. What a blessing that this Rabbi, Jesus, invited them to be His students! Jesus is not limited to the world's insight into a person's value or potential. The One who formed us knows our hearts and calls those who will to "Follow Me."

Like Jesus, our task is to make disciples according to **Matthew 28:19**. The word, "disciple" means learner, and in verse 20, Jesus explains that we make disciples "teaching them." Teaching is the goal of Christian education, and it's one of the most important ministries in the church today. Whether it's Sunday school, New Members, Bible studies, or small groups, teachers should be trained to do this work of the ministry.

Teacher training helps volunteers with skills to understand the learner's needs, methodology, and more. A seasoned resource, identified as "the best book in Christian education" by Dr. Lawrence Richards, is still being used in churches today—*Teaching Like Jesus: A Practical Guide to Christian Education in Your Church*. For details, see the Source list below.

HOW TO SAY IT

Gennesaret. geh-**NESS**-are-ett.

Draught. **DRAFT.**

Chinneroth. **CHI**-ner-oth

DAILY HOME BIBLE READINGS

MONDAY
Called to Lead Israelites from Egypt
(Exodus 3:1–12)

TUESDAY
Called to Deliver Israelites
from Midianites
(Judges 6:11–16)

WEDNESDAY
Called and Cleansed for Ministry
(Isaiah 6:1–8)

THURSDAY
Single-Mindedness
Required to Follow Jesus
(Luke 9:57–62)

FRIDAY
Repentance, Goal of God's Kindness
(Romans 2:1–11)

SATURDAY
Jesus Calls Peter to Ministry
(John 21:15–19)

SUNDAY
Don't Be Afraid to Catch People
(Luke 5:1–11)

PREPARE FOR NEXT SUNDAY

Read **Mark 2:1-12** and next week's lesson, "Called to Heal."

Sources:

Baird, W. The Interpreter's one-volume commentary on the Bible. Nashville, TN: Abingdon Press, 1971.

Blight, R. C. An Exegetical Summary of Luke 1:1-11. Dallas, TX: SIL International, 2007.

Bock, D. L. The IVP New Testament Commentary Series: Luke. Downers Grove, IL: InterVarsity Press, 1994.

Green, J. B. The New International Commentary on the New Testament: The Gospel of Luke. Grand Rapids, MI: Wm. Eerdmans, 1997.

Kapusta, Philip P. A King James Dictionary: A Resource for Understanding the Language of the King James Bible. Murrells Inlet, SC: New Covenant Press, 2012.

Marshall, H. New International Greek Testament Commentary: Commentary on Luke. Exeter, UK: Paternoster Press, 1978.

Morris, L. Tyndale New Testament Commentaries: Luke. Grand Rapids, MI: William Eerdmans, 1984.

Nolland, J. Word Biblical Commentary: Luke 1-9:20. Dallas, TX: Words Books, 1989.

The Zondervan Pictorial Bible Dictionary. Grand Rapids, MI: Zondervan Publishing Co., 1963. 296-297.

Tolbert, L. Teaching Like Jesus: A Practical Guide to Christian Education In Your Church. Grand Rapids, MI: Zondervan Publishing Co., 2000.

COMMENTS / NOTES:

_____

_____

_____

_____

_____

_____

_____

_____

_____

_____

_____

_____

_____

_____

_____

_____

_____

_____

_____

_____

CALLED TO HEAL

BIBLE BASIS: Mark 2:1-12

BIBLE TRUTH: Jesus heals the paralytic man.

MEMORY VERSE: "Whether is it easier to say to the sick of the palsy, Thy sins be forgiven thee; or to say, Arise, and take up thy bed, and walk?" (Mark 2:9, KJV)

LESSON AIM: By the end of this lesson, we will INVESTIGATE Mark's account of Jesus healing the man who was paralyzed, APPRECIATE how one's physical, emotional, social, and spiritual needs are intertwined, and PRAY for God's healing grace to touch us at our particular point of need.

BACKGROUND SCRIPTURES: Mark 2:1-12—Read and incorporate the insights gained from the Background Scriptures into your study of the lesson.

TEACHER PREPARATION

MATERIALS NEEDED: Bibles (several different versions), Quarterly Commentary/Teacher Manual, Adult Quarterly, teaching resources such as charts, worksheets/handouts, paper, pens, pencils

OTHER MATERIALS NEEDED / TEACHER'S NOTES:

_____

_____

LESSON OVERVIEW

LIFE NEED FOR TODAY'S LESSON
The limitations of human existence make genuine wholeness an elusive goal. Where can we find true healing? By declaring a paralyzed man's sins forgiven and restoring his physical health, Jesus demonstrated that God had called Jesus to heal infirmities of the soul as well as the body.

BIBLE LEARNING
Jesus demonstrates that He is the Messiah by forgiving sin and healing the sick.

BIBLE APPLICATION
Believers experience joy because of Jesus' power to forgive sins.

STUDENTS' RESPONSES
Believers are thankful for the healing of body, mind, and spirit.

LESSON SCRIPTURE

MARK 2:1-12, KJV

1 And again he entered into Capernaum after some days; and it was noised that he was in the house.

2 And straightway many were gathered together, insomuch that there was no room to receive them, no, not so much as about the door: and he preached the word unto them.

3 And they come unto him, bringing one sick of the palsy, which was borne of four.

4 And when they could not come nigh unto him for the press, they uncovered the roof where he was: and when they had broken it up, they let down the bed wherein the sick of the palsy lay.

5 When Jesus saw their faith, he said unto the sick of the palsy, Son, thy sins be forgiven thee.

6 But there was certain of the scribes sitting there, and reasoning in their hearts,

7 Why doth this man thus speak blasphemies? who can forgive sins but God only?

8 And immediately when Jesus perceived in his spirit that they so reasoned within themselves, he said unto them, Why reason ye these things in your hearts?

9 Whether is it easier to say to the sick of the palsy, Thy sins be forgiven thee; or to say, Arise, and take up thy bed, and walk?

10 But that ye may know that the Son of man hath power on earth to forgive sins, (he saith to the sick of the palsy,)

11 I say unto thee, Arise, and take up thy bed, and go thy way into thine house.

12 And immediately he arose, took up the bed, and went forth before them all; insomuch that they were all amazed, and glorified God, saying, We never saw it on this fashion.

BIBLICAL DEFINITIONS

A. Perceived (Mark 2:8) *epiginosko* (Gk.)— To know, recognize, or acknowledge; to be fully acquainted with

B. Amazed (v. 12) *existemi* (Gk.)—To be put out of one's wits, be beside oneself; to be astounded, astonished, or insane

LIGHT ON THE WORD

Palsy. This disability is due to the loss of motor function of muscles or nerves. It refers to all forms of paralysis. The term "palsy" translates the Greek word *paralutikos* (pah-rah-loo-tih-**KAHSS**) from which we derive the English words paralytic and paralysis. The man in this week's Scripture is paralyzed and is unable to walk. Other accounts of paralysis appear in the book of Matthew, which records the Capernaum centurion asking Jesus to heal his servant of paralysis (**Matthew 8:5-6**), and in Acts where the apostles healed those who suffered from this condition (**Acts 8:7; 9:33-34**).

Scribes. Often called lawyers, doctors, or teachers of the Law (**Matthew 22:35**), they were neither a Jewish sect or a party, nor were they priests. The title, scribe, referred to their capacity as transcribers of the Hebrew Bible. They would copy the entire Old Testament by hand onto new scrolls when a new copy was needed. This careful, precise copying of the Law, Prophets, and Writings gave them extensive knowledge of the Scriptures. Mark often presents the scribes in the company of the Pharisees and chief priests.

TEACHING THE BIBLE LESSON

LIFE NEED FOR TODAY'S LESSON

AIM: Students will marvel at the expanse of Jesus' ministry.

INTRODUCTION

The Miracle Worker

The news of Jesus—the miracle-worker—spread throughout Capernaum. This was an exciting time. The community had never experienced a healer and teacher like Jesus. No wonder **Mark 1:32-33** speaks of the townspeople bringing all the sick and demon-possessed to Jesus! And in Jesus' great compassion, He healed every one of them! After this exhausting time of ministry, the next morning, Jesus left to be alone with the Father.

The Scriptures do not tell the length of Jesus' solitude, but the disciples' appearance shortened His time alone. Jesus was not irritated by the disciples' interruption. He told them that He must preach in other places: "Let us go into the next towns, that I may preach there also: for therefore came I forth" (from **Mark 1:38**). Jesus knew His mission was to spread the Gospel to everyone, so He traveled to other towns performing miracles and healings, demonstrating that He was the Messiah.

BIBLE LEARNING

AIM: Students will acknowledge the faith of friends in the account of the paralytic.

I. JESUS PREACHES (MARK 2:1-4)

When Jesus entered Capernaum (**v. 1**), He preached "the word," meaning the Gospel of God's kingdom. Mark's description of the enthusiastic crowd that gathered suggests that it filled the house, jammed the doorway, and spilled out into the street. What a tribute to the ministry of Jesus!

Four men carrying their friend, "one sick of the palsy," joined the crowd, but they could not get into the house through the door. They carried the paralyzed man up the outside stairway to the roof of the house. Oriental house structures of the time had one or two stories built in a rectangle or square. There was one door that opened into an open space called the porch, which had a stairway that led to the roof. These friends saw the roof as a means to reach Jesus. They tore the roof open and lowered the man on his bed down through the opening where Jesus stood preaching. What a scene!

1 And again he entered into Capernaum after some days; and it was noised that he was in the house. 2 And straightway many were gathered together, insomuch that there was no room to receive them, no, not so much as about the door: and he preached the word unto them.

Verse 1 states that Jesus "was in the house." Many scholars assume this is Peter's house, which became His headquarters in Capernaum (**Matthew 4:13; 9:1; Mark 1:21, 29**). It does seem the natural base of operations since Jesus had been there previously, and Peter was a leader among the disciples.

People were drawn to Jesus—to His presence, His words, His wisdom, His actions, His attitude, and the grace of God that rested upon Him as the Son of God. The crowds wanted to be close to Jesus, to experience His presence, to listen to His words, to hear His voice. They wanted to see Jesus. The Lord Jesus preached the Word of God to them. Mark had previously told us that Jesus' message was of the coming kingdom and repentance. He preached God's wisdom, God's counsel, and God's compassion. Jesus was both the Messenger and the Message. Jesus was a living example of what He preached and taught. His lifestyle was never a contradiction of His Word. Jesus was the living testimony of all that He preached and taught. Jesus is the Word of God!

3 And they come unto him, bringing one sick of the palsy, which was borne of four. 4 And when they could not come nigh unto him for the press, they uncovered the roof where he was: and when they had broken it up, they let down the bed wherein the sick of the palsy lay.

The roofs of Palestinian houses were flat with railings so that people would not fall off (**Deuteronomy 22:8; Judges 16:27; 2 Samuel 11:2**). On top of some houses, there was access via outside stairs. These types of houses are still common in the northern part of the African continent, especially in northern Nigeria. Houses there are built flat-roofed with mud and wooden beams covered with thatch.

Four friends are determined to get to Jesus, and they carry the sick man up the outside stairs to the roof of the house. They dig through the thatch or roof tiles (**Luke 5:19**) and lower the man in front of Jesus. There the sick man lay at Jesus' feet.

SEARCH THE SCRIPTURES
QUESTION 1
Why is the four friends' creativity—in the face of an obstacle like the closed door—encouraging?

Answers will vary.

QUESTION 2
Share about a time you have worked hard to help a friend "meet" God.

Answers will vary.

LIGHT ON THE WORD
Four Friends
We do not know much about these four friends who carried the paralyzed man to Christ, but we recognize their great faith. They believed that the Lord Jesus could and would heal their friend of this illness, or they would not have made such an effort to bring him to the Lord. These four friends were selfless; they put this man and his needs before any concern for themselves or material things. Their actions in tearing up the roof were not an example of reckless destruction of property because a roof can be repaired. These four friends understood that this man's healing was much more critical than any roof. Their actions remind us that people are always much more important than things.

How refreshing, encouraging, and uplifting it is when we have Christian friends who touch our lives with their faith. Friends who love the Lord and who love and support us in prayer and encouragement are special gifts to us from God. Friends who will sacrifice themselves on our behalf are precious. When we have genuine Christian friends, we have treasures that are more valuable than gold.

II. JESUS PARDONS (vv. 5-9)

Jesus knows this extraordinary action stemmed from exceptional faith. He pardons the crippled man's sin. The teachers of the Law say nothing, but they are outraged about Jesus forgiving sins. Based on Old Testament laws (**Exodus 34:6–7**), the scribes knew that only God had the authority to forgive sins. In their view, Jesus had committed blasphemy (**Leviticus 24:15-16**), which was a serious charge punishable by death. Even though the scribes do not voice their concerns aloud, Jesus knows their thoughts, which serves as further proof that He is the all-knowing, all-powerful God. Jesus declares His authority as One who is able not only to heal but also to forgive sins. Jesus' words convey to the scribes that forgiving sins is the same as healing. Since Jesus can heal, as the scribes had seen Him do, then He can also forgive sins.

5 When Jesus saw their faith, he said unto the sick of palsy, Son, thy sins be forgiven thee.

Jesus is not angry about the hole in the roof. Instead, the Lord Jesus acknowledges "their" faith, the plural indicating not just the man with paralysis, but also the four who brought him to Jesus. The four friends demonstrate their faith by their extreme efforts to get to Jesus. In turn, Jesus responds to their faith by speaking words of forgiveness to the paralyzed man, whom He calls "son" (Gk. *teknon*, **TEK**-non). This address shows the affection of the loving care of a father. A teacher's followers would also use this term. Since the man and his helpers have already shown their great faith in Jesus' ability to heal and their awareness of their great need for Jesus specifically, Jesus does not hesitate to include the man among His followers.

Of course, the man or his friends are not looking for forgiveness, and Jesus' pronouncement does not mean that the man

is particularly sinful. Forgiveness illustrates the common belief in the Old Testament that every suffering is rooted in man's alienation from God. To Jesus, the man's most profound need is the healing of the soul (conversion and the forgiveness of sins). Jesus, therefore, calls the people's attention to this need by proclaiming forgiveness. This single act provokes controversy and conflict against Jesus among the scribes and Jewish authorities. It is also, according to Mark's record, the beginning of the conflict in Christ's ministry on earth.

6 But there were certain of the scribes sitting there, and reasoning in their hearts, 7 Why doth this man thus speak blasphemies? who can forgive sins but God only?

Among the crowd gathered in the house to hear Jesus are some scribes—"teachers of religious law" (**Mark 1:22, NLT**). Their purpose in coming is not evident, but they may have been curious about the nature of His teaching as compared with their own (**1:22**) or the miracles He had already performed. At other points in the Gospel accounts, the motive of the religious leaders is to trap Jesus on theological issues. Here, as Jesus forgives, the scribes have their opportunity.

The scribes were immediately critical, thinking that Jesus did not have the authority to forgive sins. To forgive sins was blasphemy since the forgiveness of sin is a task for God alone. For a mere human to claim such power is heresy. Blasphemy is the charge they eventually bring against Jesus when they demand His execution on the Cross (**Mark 14:64**).

8 And immediately when Jesus perceived in his spirit that they so reasoned within themselves, he said

unto them, Why reason ye these things in your hearts? 9 Whether is it easier to say to the sick of the palsy, Thy sins be forgiven thee; or to say, Arise, and take up thy bed, and walk?

Through the Spirit, Jesus immediately discerns their thoughts. Both actions (vv. 7-8) are simultaneous, as fast as the thoughts themselves. Mark uses the adverb "immediately," *eutheus* (Gk. yew-**THAY**-oce), a word he uses frequently in his Gospel, which can also be translated "forthwith" or "straightway." Mark portrays Christ's ministry as one of action.

As the scribes contemplate this in their hearts, Jesus through the Holy Ghost perceives it. The word "perceived" is from the Greek verb *epiginosko* (eh-pee-gee-**NOCE**-koh) meaning to recognize or acknowledge. It has the idea of not just being acquainted with, but being fully acquainted with or having full knowledge of. Even though the scribes do not say a word, Jesus hears their thoughts—further proof that Christ is the omniscient God. Although they have not expressed their thoughts openly, through His question, Jesus implicitly makes them know who He is. Only God can know and discern the inner thoughts of people.

Humanly speaking, to the scribes, both forgiving sins and healing the man are impossible. Jesus criticizes the people for their unbelief. They have already seen Him perform healings, but they still think He cannot do the equally impossible task of forgiving sins.

SEARCH THE SCRIPTURES

QUESTION 3
Why is it wise to have friends who are full of faith?

Answers will vary.

QUESTION 4
Why is it equally wise to exclude doubters from our circle of friends?

Answers will vary.

LIGHT ON THE WORD

Jesus Is The Son Of God
By forgiving the person with paralysis, Jesus demonstrates that He is not a mere human.The doctrine of the Church Of God In Christ explains his divinity the following way.

We believe that Jesus Christ is the Son of God, the Second person in the Godhead of the Trinity or Triune Godhead. We believe that Jesus was and is eternal in his person and nature as the Son of God who was with God in the beginning of creation (St. John 1:1). We believe that Jesus Christ was born of a virgin called Mary according to the scripture (St. Matthew 1:18), thus giving rise to our fundamental belief in the Virgin Birth and to all of the miraculous events surrounding the phenomenon (St. Matthew 1:18-25). We believe that Jesus Christ became the "suffering servant" to man; this suffering servant came seeking to redeem man from sin and to reconcile him back to God, his Father (Romans 5:10). We believe that Jesus Christ is standing now as mediator between God and man (I Timothy 2:5).

Jesus is not the Father. The Father is not the Son. And the Son is not the Holy Spirit. Each Person of the Godhead is fully God and in unity with the other Divine Persons. God is one unity, one Divine being, yet each eternal Person within the Trinity plays a unique role in the united being of God.

III. JESUS HEALS PARALYSIS (vv. 10-12)

Jesus turns His attention to the paralytic and commands him, "Arise, and take up thy bed, and go thy way into thine house" (**v. 11**). The healing verified Jesus' claim to grant forgiveness. Since the healing was real and impossible for anyone but God, the claim to forgive sins is also real. The paralyzed man immediately got up, took up his bed, and walked out in full view of the crowd. This amazed everyone, and they praised God—they had never seen anything like this!

10 But that you may know that the Son of man hath power on earth to forgive sins, (he saith to the sick of the palsy,) 11 I say unto thee, Arise, and take up thy bed, and go thy way into thine house.

The Lord Jesus has both the power to forgive sin and the power to heal. A grateful man received Christ's forgiveness and the gift of wholeness in his body.

Jesus reveals His true identity as the "Son of man" to the scribes. The "Son of man" is the title Christ most often applies to Himself. It is an Aramaic way to refer to the "everyman," but it is also a declaration of His divinity because it is an allusion to ancient prophecy (**Daniel 7:13**). To demonstrate His authority to forgive sins—contrary to their belief—He heals the person with paralysis.

The paralytic man shows surprisingly little agency in this healing account. Usually, Jesus talks with the sick person about if and how to heal them. Jesus, however, has already seen that the man with palsy has faith in Him. Christ's actions now intend to grow the faith of the scribes. The man's physical and outward healing corroborates His claim of authority to forgive sins. It makes the crowd realize that since He can do the miracle of healing, which they can see, He can also do the other miracle of forgiveness, which they cannot see.

12 And immediately he arose, took up the bed, and went forth before them all; insomuch that they were all amazed, and glorified God, saying, We never saw it on this fashion.

The Lord Jesus, with authority and power, commanded the paralyzed man to arise, take up his bed, and go home. The man obeyed. His obedience was an act of faith. Through his faith and obedience, he received his healing. The response of the people who witnessed this miracle was amazement, and they glorified God. This miracle and others pointed people to the Lord and the salvation He provided.

The sick man is restored not just to health, but to strength. Even after a short time without the use of one's legs, muscles begin to shrink and weaken. Jesus heals the damaged nerves causing palsy in the man's legs and also strengthens his legs so that he can "immediately" stand, lift his bedding, and walk through the crowded room.

Everyone in the crowd is astonished, including the teachers who challenged Jesus' authority. The word "amazed" comes from the Greek verb *existemi* (ex-**ISS**-tay-mee) which means to be put out of one's wits, be beside oneself, to be astounded, or astonished, or to become astounded.

The reaction of the crowd moves from being "amazed" to praise. They praise God because never before have they seen anything like this!

SEARCH THE SCRIPTURES

QUESTION 5

Imagine that you were there. What might have been your reactions from the moment someone broke up the roof to the moment the paralyzed man walked home?

Answers will vary.

QUESTION 6

Have you ever prayed for healing? If you feel comfortable doing so, briefly share your testimony.

Answers will vary.

LIGHT ON THE WORD

God Still Heals

Every healing that takes place is cause for rejoicing and praising God. God still heals, but we all know instances where healing didn't occur. Sometimes in the face of our illness, our faith demonstrates God's higher purpose (**John 9**) and our relationship with Him. Our faith, despite the absence of physical healing, can recognize the grace of God's peace and strength even in our weakened state. God's healing may be physical, emotional, or spiritual. Even in the absence of healing (**2 Corinthians 12:7**), we must remember that His grace is sufficient, and our faith is the trademark of our relationship with Him—a relationship based on the forgiveness of our sins and reconciliation with our God.

The main thrust of this biblical account is not rooted in Jesus' healing of the helpless paralytic.

The emphasis is on Jesus' ability to forgive sins. Sin is the sick man's primary problem—and, indeed, all of humanity's! Jesus first declares forgiveness and, in so doing, proclaims the presence of the Kingdom of God to humanity, which is the goal of His earthly mission.

BIBLE APPLICATION

AIM: Students will continue to trust God for their healing.

Illness and infirmity in body, mind, and soul afflict everyone today. May those who have not yet found physical healing continue seeking it by faith. Paul tells us that God comforts us so that we can comfort others (**2 Corinthians 1:4**).

The testimony of God's presence in your life at a time when healing or deliverance was needed provides an opportunity to share how God sustained you through that time. Whether He has brought you out or continues to help you through, sharing with other hurting people helps them know they are not alone.

STUDENTS' RESPONSES

AIM: Students will pray for a friend who needs healing.

Think of someone you know who is suffering from a physical illness. Take that person to an elder, or ask an elder to come to the hospital or home to anoint with oil, lay hands, and pray in faith. If the physical illness continues, there is more to pray for than a cure. Pray for God's grace and increased faith.

Make a list of the times God has healed you physically, emotionally, or spiritually. Reflect on how that healing changed your life and deepened your faith. If you are still awaiting healing, reflect on the blessings He has given you during your situation.

PRAYER

Father, You loved us so much that You sent Your Son, Jesus into the world and gave us the Holy Spirit to live in us and teach us. We so appreciate all that You have provided, including faith-filled friends who pray for us. Thank You for loving us so much. In the precious Name of Jesus, we pray. Amen.

DIG A LITTLE DEEPER

Divine healing is a core doctrine of the Church Of God In Christ. Here is the statement from www.cogic.org: "The Church of God in Christ believes in and practices Divine Healing. It is a commandment of Jesus to the Apostles (**St. Mark 16:18**). Jesus affirms his teachings on healing by explaining to His disciples, who were to be Apostles, that healing the afflicted is by faith (**St. Luke 9:40-41**). Therefore, we believe that healing by faith in God has scriptural support and ordained authority. St. James' writings in his epistle encourage Elders to pray for the sick, lay hands upon them and to anoint them with oil, and that prayers with faith shall heal the sick and the Lord shall raise them up. Healing is still practiced widely and frequently in the Church of God in Christ, and testimonies of healing in our Church testify to this fact." And the Church says, Amen!

HOW TO SAY IT

Capernaum. kah-**PEER**-nah-um.

Palsy. **PALL**-zee.

DAILY HOME BIBLE READINGS

MONDAY
Peace and Healing Will Come
(Isaiah 57:14–21)

TUESDAY
Healed by Christ's Wounds
(1 Peter 2:18–25)

WEDNESDAY
Canaanite Daughter Healed by
Mother's Faith
(Matthew 15:21–28)

THURSDAY
Anoint Sick with Oil and Prayer
(James 5:13–16)

FRIDAY
Woman Healed by Her Faith
(Mark 5:21–34)

SATURDAY
The Sick Need a Physician
(Mark 2:13–17)

SUNDAY
Jesus Heals and Forgives
the Paralytic
(Mark 2:1–12)

PREPARE FOR NEXT SUNDAY

Read **John 17:14-24** and next week's lesson, "Called as the Intercessor."

Sources:
Thayer, Joseph Henry. *A Greek-English Lexicon of the New Testament.* New York: American Book Company, 1996.
Strong, James. *The New Strong's Exhaustive Concordance of the Bible.* Nashville, TN: Thomas Nelson, 2003.
Vine, W.E. *Vine's Complete Expository Dictionary of Old and New Testament Words.* Nashville, TN: Thomas Nelson, 1996.

CALLED AS THE INTERCESSOR

BIBLE BASIS: John 17:14-24

BIBLE TRUTH: Jesus looked down the halls of eternity and prayed for you.

MEMORY VERSE: "Neither pray I for these alone, but for them also which shall believe on me through their word" (John 17:20).

LESSON AIM: By the end of this lesson, we will EXPLORE Jesus' intercessory prayer for His disciples, LONG for Jesus' prayer to be answered more fully in their lives and the church, and PRAY for others and work for unity in the body of Christ.

BACKGROUND SCRIPTURES: John 17:14-24 —Read and incorporate the insights gained from the Background Scriptures into your study of the lesson.

TEACHER PREPARATION

MATERIALS NEEDED: Bibles (several different versions), Quarterly Commentary/Teacher Manual, Adult Quarterly, teaching resources such as charts, worksheets/handouts, paper, pens, pencils

OTHER MATERIALS NEEDED / TEACHER'S NOTES:

_____

_____

LESSON OVERVIEW

LIFE NEED FOR TODAY'S LESSON
People often look for ways to appeal for assistance on behalf of others. How can people respond to the urge to intercede in a meaningful manner? Jesus' prayer for His disciples serves as a call to use intercessory prayer for the sake of others.

BIBLE LEARNING
Jesus prays for His disciples and for those who will believe on His Name.

BIBLE APPLICATION
Believers examine the High Priestly prayer.

STUDENTS' RESPONSES
Believers pray for one another.

LESSON SCRIPTURE

JOHN 17:14-24, KJV

14 I have given them thy word; and the world hath hated them, because they are not of the world, even as I am not of the world.

15 I pray not that thou shouldest take them out of the world, but that thou shouldest keep them from the evil.

16 They are not of the world, even as I am not of the world.

17 Sanctify them through thy truth: thy word is truth.

18 As thou hast sent me into the world, even so have I also sent them into the world.

19 And for their sakes I sanctify myself, that they also might be sanctified through the truth.

20 Neither pray I for these alone, but for them also which shall believe on me through their word;

21 That they all may be one; as thou, Father, art in me, and I in thee, that they also may be one in us: that the world may believe that thou hast sent me.

22 And the glory which thou gavest me I have given them; that they may be one, even as we are one:

23 I in them, and thou in me, that they may be made perfect in one; and that the world may know that thou hast sent me, and hast loved them, as thou hast loved me.

24 Father, I will that they also, whom thou hast given me, be with me where I am; that they may behold my glory, which thou hast given me: for thou lovedst me before the foundation of the world.

BIBLICAL DEFINITIONS

A. Sanctify (**John 17:17**) *hagiazo* (Gk.)—To set apart for holiness, to be separated from the profane for sacred use; to consecrate.

B. Perfect (**v. 23**) *teleioo* (Gk.)—To make complete and one, to thoroughly finish, to come to the end

LIGHT ON THE WORD

God as Jesus' Father. Jesus' relationship with the Father is unique because He is the eternal Son of God. Jesus expressed His intimate relationship to God by referring to Him as "Abba" (**Mark 14:36**). Abba is an Aramaic word that denotes a warm sense of intimacy. On several occasions, Jesus spoke of God as "My Father" (**Matthew 7:21**; **10:32**; **16:17**). The personal pronoun is expressive of their relationship. The claim that Jesus had a unique Father-Son relationship with God was shocking to the religious leaders of Jesus' time. His claim not only violated their traditions, but also the Jewish leaders understood that Jesus was making Himself God's equal.

The World. In the New Testament specifically, the Greek word *kosmos* (**KOS**-mos) carries a variety of meanings. In some verses, it has a positive denotation of all humanity (**John 3:16**: "the world"). John most often uses it to refer to the realm of sin and human affairs in alienation and opposition to God (**1 John 4:5**; **5:19**). John declares the nature of the world is ruled by lust and pride and dominated by Satan, God's enemy. The world's system has an inherent hatred toward God. In the end, the world and its wares are passing away. However, those who believe in Christ and obey God's Word will abide forever (cf. **2:8**).

TEACHING THE BIBLE LESSON

LIFE NEED FOR TODAY'S LESSON

AIM: Students will contrast the model prayer with the High Priestly Prayer.

INTRODUCTION

The High Priestly Prayer

The prayer in **Matthew 6:9-13** is commonly called "The Lord's Prayer." However, that prayer is a model for the prayers of believers. The true Lord's Prayer is the prayer of **John 17**, which is Jesus' farewell prayer for His disciples. In the prayer of **Matthew 6**, Jesus explains what His disciples should desire for themselves. In the prayer of **John 17**, Jesus petitions God on behalf of His disciples.

Jesus and His disciples had just finished eating the Passover meal. And "Jesus knew that his hour was come that he should depart out of this world unto the Father" (from **John 13:1**). Jesus gave the disciples their final instructions. He told them of the coming betrayal, going to the Father to prepare a place for them, and the coming of the Holy Ghost (**John 13-16**).

After completing His final teaching, called the "Upper Room Discourse," Jesus offered up His most extended recorded prayer, called the "High Priestly Prayer." Jesus prayed for His disciples either in the Upper Room, on the way to, or in the Garden of Gethsemane.

BIBLE LEARNING

AIM: Students will identify themselves as disciples of Jesus Christ.

I. THE BELIEVERS' PROTECTION (JOHN 17:14-16)

In this final prayer before His Passion, Jesus petitions God for His followers. The Lord realizes that His earthly ministry is drawing to an end. Soon He will return to His rightful place in heaven, so He commits His followers to the Father's care. Jesus affirms that He has completed part of His mission by giving the disciples the Father's Word. Jesus Himself is the Word

of God. By His teaching, preaching, and His holy presence, He has imparted the Father's Word to His followers.

Although believers are separate from the world, Christ does not expect disciples to withdraw from the world. Instead, He prays that we are protected from the world's evil influences. The "evil one" is Satan, the devil, who always seeks to drag people away from God. Though the disciples will be in the world, they belong elsewhere (namely Heaven), just like Jesus Himself. Their allegiance and citizenship have changed to the Kingdom of Heaven.

14 I have given them thy word; and the world hath hated them, because they are not of the world, even as I am not of the world

This section of Jesus' prayer begins with His assurance that He has imparted "thy word" to the disciples. Repeatedly throughout His ministry, Jesus says that His teachings are straight from God the Father (**John 5:19; 8:28; 12:49**). Jesus' teaching has not been His own, but God the Father's. Now at the end of His time on earth, Jesus' mission to preach the Gospel is complete. He has revealed Himself—and therefore, the Father—to the disciples.

Earlier in Jesus' ministry, He acknowledges that the world hates Him (**John 7:7**). Jesus was a witness against the world's evil. No one likes to have their flaws pointed out, especially when they believe they are doing well. Because the world sets itself against Jesus, it reflects the need for Jesus' correction. Instead of listening to Jesus' Word and improving, the world stubbornly ignores Jesus and hates that He even mentions its flaws.

Jesus will assert several commonalities between Him and His disciples and this verse contains the first one. The disciples do not belong to this world any more than Christ does. It is easy to see why the Messiah would not feel He belongs to this sinful world. He is patient, kind, powerful, loving, and self-sacrificing. His soul is the stuff of heaven. Here Jesus says all those reasons He does not belong to this world also apply to His followers.

15 I pray not that thou shouldest take them out of the world, but that thou shouldest keep them from the evil. 16 They are not of the world, even as I am not of the world.

Take note of the tone of the prayer. Jesus is not asking that God should take them away from the world, but rather that He should protect them. Jesus does not pray that God should destroy Satan, nor that the disciples should die and leave this world to escape the onslaught of the evil one, nor that they should be separated and given a different world of their own so that they would be free from evil. Rather He prays that God should protect them from the temptations and persecutions that await them. He prays that, although they are in a world that is full of evil, they may live as lights and examples of God.

Given His fast-approaching departure, Jesus specifically prays for the disciples' protection from the "evil one," which refers undoubtedly to Satan, the prince of the world (**John 12:31; 14:30; 16:11**). Jesus, realizing the power and presence of Satan and his work against the people of God, prays for divine protection and strength.

Evil comes in many forms, so Jesus prays His disciples would be protected from all evil. But evil is not just an amorphous, chaotic, mindless force of fallen nature. A malevolent spiritual enemy is at work to oppose Christ's work. That enemy sets himself against Christ's disciples in many ways.

Jesus identifies with the disciples, attesting to their unity and the disciples' holiness as He has done previously (**15:3, 19**). He says, "They are not of the world" as He is also not of the world. John records Jesus' words about the world (*kosmos*), which dominate this prayer. There are many ways to use the word *kosmos*, whether to refer to all the people of the world, the globe itself, or sinful humanity at odds with heaven. Throughout His ministry, as recorded by John, Jesus uses the word *kosmos* to refer to all people. When we look at the context, we see those people need saving. Here in the final days of Jesus' ministry, the meaning shifts to a picture of the sinful systems of humanity that have set themselves against God and His workers. Three times Jesus refers to the "prince of this world (*kosmos*)," implying that the sinful systems of humanity are evil because they are merely following their leader, Satan.

However, Christ contends, neither He nor His disciples are from that sinful world. Christ again confirms that He and we (His disciples) share a unity, which implies disunion with the world. Because we are not one with the world, the world recognizes Christ's disciples as its enemy.

SEARCH THE SCRIPTURES

QUESTION 1
What emotions do you sense as Jesus is praying?

Answers will vary.

QUESTION 2

If you could only give one last prayer for your children, grandchildren, or a group you lead, what would you pray for them?

Answers will vary.

LIGHT ON THE WORD

In . . . But Not *Of* The World

This small community of believers—the twelve disciples, along with the women who also followed Jesus—would experience persecution. Still, Jesus does not wish the Father to remove the disciples from the hostility. The only way to accomplish this would be to bring the disciples home to Heaven immediately. Escaping the world's hostility would fulfill the disciples' unity with Christ and the Father, but it would leave the world to its own devices and deprive the rest of humanity of learning to follow God.

Paul faced a similar quandary in his ministry, telling the Philippian church that he had "a desire to depart, and to be with Christ; which is far better" (**Philippians 1:23**). However, he was needed here on earth to continue his ministry to churches, like the one in Philippi.

Jesus asks the Father to protect His disciples from the "evil one." Sometimes, in the face of persecution and death, it seems that the disciples were not protected at all. Many died a martyr's death. In areas of our world today, Christians are being massacred, and it may also seem that God's people are not protected. However, their protection is guaranteed! Believers are the apple of the Lord's eye, and whatever persecution we encounter, God is always in control. Jesus says we are blessed when persecuted for His sake (**Matthew 5:11–12**).

Since we do not belong to this world, God will not leave us alone.

II. THE BELIEVERS' SANCTIFICATION (vv. 17-19)

Jesus' second petition is for sanctification: "Sanctify them through thy truth" (**v. 17**). To sanctify means to set apart for God and His holy purposes. Every believer is set apart to carry on the work of Christ (**v. 18**). Each Christian has been appointed some divine task and equipped to carry it out. God sent Jesus with a specific mission to enlighten all humanity that involved a great deal of courage, prayer, and self-sacrifice. This is what He expects from us and for which we are prepared and personally "sanctified."

Jesus resisted all temptation so that He could successfully carry out His spiritual responsibility. He did this so that others "might be sanctified through the truth." The truth is God's active Word that must be obeyed. Jesus, in His incarnation, was God's truth (**14:6**); His followers know the truth (**8:32**) and abide in truth (**8:44**). For their sakes, Jesus has consecrated Himself as a living sacrifice standing in the gap on our behalf.

17 Sanctify them through thy truth: thy word is truth. 18 As thou hast sent me into the world, even so have I also sent them into the world. 19 And for their sakes I sanctify myself, that they also might be sanctified through the truth.

Jesus makes another specific request, asking God to sanctify the disciples. The word "sanctify" is the Greek word, *hagiazo* (haw-gee-**ODD**-zo). It means to set apart, to be separated from profane things for sacred use. It has the idea of consecrating, or being consecrated or making holy. The idea is similar to being separate from the world, a concept Jesus stated in **verse 16**.

Jesus prays that God will continue to keep the disciples separate from the world through the Word of God, which is equated with truth. The Word refers to the teachings of Christ. The twelve and the women are to be separate to continue His ministry on earth (**v. 18**).

As the Father commissioned Jesus to the ministry, so Jesus commissions the disciples to minister the word of truth in the world (cf **Matthew 28:20; Mark 15:15-20; John 14:12; 20:21**). For this purpose and the benefit of the disciples, Jesus says that He separates Himself.

Jesus consecrates Himself to fulfill the work of redemption. Therefore, Jesus is an example for believers to follow (See **1 John 1:7; Ephesians 5:26**). The Father sent Jesus into the world, and now Jesus sends His disciples into this same world. The Greek word for "sent" is *apostello* (ah-poe-STEL-low), which means "to order to go to an appointed place" or "to send away." The English word "apostle" is from this same root. The disciples were consecrated to serve as Apostles—the "sent ones." With the impending Cross on His mind, Jesus sets a basis for the disciples' obedience later by His resolve to do the Father's will, which means death on the Cross. Jesus sets Himself apart, or sanctifies Himself, to perform the redemptive work on the Cross. The beneficiaries of that work also set themselves apart from the world that hates them. Jesus demonstrates to the disciples that the Father's will reigns supreme, and the disciples' best response to God's will is to willingly present to God their lives.

SEARCH THE SCRIPTURES

QUESTION 3
Why does Jesus pray the disciples will be sanctified?

The disciples have much work to do in spreading the Gospel. They have been set apart for this task.

QUESTION 4
How have you sanctified yourself to God's purpose? How do you manifest that promise in everyday life?

Answers will vary.

LIGHT ON THE WORD
We Are Sanctified
As believers, we are sanctified, or set apart, by truth. Jesus prays "thy word is truth" (**v. 17**). Christ has given the disciples God's Word (**v. 14**) and in so doing, He has completely prepared believers with truth, which is how we are sanctified.

The purpose of sanctification is to complete the work God has entrusted to us. And, through the Holy Ghost, God has given us the spiritual resources we need to carry out our task. Our assignments differ, but the entire Christian community is set apart as an apostolic community sent out by Christ to be His witnesses in the world.

III. THE BELIEVERS' UNITY (vv. 20-24)

This prayer can be summed up as a desire for a unity that mimics the unity Jesus has with the Father. Up to this point, Jesus has focused His prayer primarily on His disciples. Now He looks to the future and prays for the universal Church throughout the ages. The Father and Son provide the best example of Christian unity (**John 17:21**). Christians will find themselves united with each other as they unite with Christ.

The glory of Christ unites Christians through our common salvation, which serves as a sign to the world that Christ came from God and lives within us. Jesus asks that the unity of believers would show the world that Jesus was sent by the Father and would cause the world to believe in Him as Savior. All believers should join with Christ in praying that God be glorified and that believers everywhere be protected, sanctified, and unified.

20 Neither pray I for these alone, but for them also which shall believe on me through their word; 21 That they all may be one; as thou, Father, art in me, and I in thee, that they also may be one in us: that the world may believe that thou hast sent me.

In **verses 21-24**, Jesus concentrates on unity in the Body of Christ. The unity to which the Church aspires is exemplified in the unity between the Father and the Son. Jesus makes this ardent request four times in this section and once in **verse 11**.

The Church's manifest oneness gives public confirmation both of their relationship with Jesus and the relationship of Jesus with the Father. This unity is a witness of God's love to the world, and that is how the Church multiplies. Such love is not by human effort, but possible only through God's power. The Church cannot be complete as a body if there is a lack of unity. Jesus offers an antidote for the world's rejection of Christ's authority and purpose on earth—and that is unity in the Church. If Christians want the world to

know God, then they must determine to be one as God and Christ are One.

22 And the glory which thou gavest me I have given them; that they may be one, even as we are one: 23 I in them, and thou in me, that they may be made perfect in one; and that the world may know that thou hast sent me, and hast loved them, as thou hast loved me.

Not only do we share Christ's otherworldly origins and belonging, but Jesus says we also share in His glory. John often speaks of the glory of God and Christ. As early as his opening summary, John says the disciples saw Jesus' glory, "the glory as of the only begotten of the Father" (**John 1:14**) as Christ performed His miracles (**John 2:11, 11:4**). Jesus says this is the glory which He shared with the Father "before the world was" (**John 17:5**), and John sees the glory of God giving light to the New Jerusalem (**Revelation 21:23**).

These two verses clarify that the glory of God is tied closely with His presence. The glory of the believers is their relationship with one another and with Christ and the Father.

It is in oneness that the Church will "be made perfect (Gk. *teleioo*, teh-lay-**OH**-oh) in one." Being one does not mean that the Church will be without fault. The word perfect means completed or thorough, so Jesus prays that our unity would be thoroughly accomplished as we receive His glory. Jesus dwells in us as the Father dwells in Him. Unity in the Church not only helps the world believe God sent Jesus (cf. **v. 21**), but it also shows that God loves us as He loves Jesus.

24 Father, I will that they also, whom thou hast given me, be with me where I am; that they may behold my glory, which thou hast given me: for thou lovedst me before the foundation of the world.

Jesus appeals to His pre-existence here. It is important to remember that Christ did not suddenly appear for the first time in Bethlehem. He is co-eternal with the other two Persons of the Trinity. Jesus is the same deity as the God seen in the Old Testament.

Jesus concludes this prayer by requesting that all persons that the Father has given Him may be with Him where He is (**John 14:1-3**), which is Heaven. When Christ's followers join Him in Heaven, they will see the glory which Christ had before the world was made and before His incarnation. The believers' destiny to behold the glory of Christ is assured because Jesus, our High Priest, makes this request. Jesus closes His earnest prayer with a request for companionship. When Jesus died on the Cross, He reconciled the entire creation with God. The centerpiece of this act is the reconciliation between God and humanity. In interceding for His disciples, Jesus prayed that his followers, in this present world, would seek and experience reconciliation with each other, just as they have been reconciled with God.

SEARCH THE SCRIPTURES

QUESTION 5
What can we do to achieve unity in the Church?

Answers will vary.

QUESTION 6
How has the lack of unity in the Church, the Body of Christ, contributed to the world rejecting the Gospel?

Answers will vary.

LIGHT ON THE WORD
Jesus Prayed For You
On His way to Calvary, Jesus prayed for you. Jesus looked down the halls of eternity, saw you, and prayed for you with the same intensity and earnest passion that He prayed for the twelve and for the women who were his followers.

You—specifically, individually, personally-matter. The person you are, the gifts God has given you, and the purpose for which God sanctified you means that you are uniquely cherished by God. With drops of blood mixed with water on His brow, Jesus poured out His love for you by making His final prayer on earth a prayer for you.

Child of God, lift your head! Straighten your back! Stand tall! Jesus suffered, and He endured betrayal and rejection because He had *you* on His mind.

BIBLE APPLICATION

AIM: Students will be active participants in the unity of the Church.

Many of the problems in our communities would be solved by a united effort on the part of God's people. What effect might such unity have on crime, immorality, a disproportionate number of African American children in foster care, and other social ills?

STUDENTS' RESPONSES

AIM: Students will identify a specific area for which to pray.

This week select a community or church problem that you want God to answer. Then choose a prayer partner. You and your prayer partner will spend at least ten minutes each day praying for this problem. Be prepared to report back to class next week with your experiences.

PRAYER

Oh Father, we present our lives to You in consecration and obedience. It's difficult to imagine that You love us as You love Jesus, and Jesus loves us as He loves You. Amazing love! May we love one another and do everything we can to bring unity to Your Church. In the Name of Jesus, we pray. Amen.

DIG A LITTLE DEEPER

Do you know who you are, who you really are? Why not trade poor self-esteem for a healthy dose of God-esteem? Why not see yourself through the eyes of God who fashioned you and called you to be His own? If you are struggling with feelings of inadequacy or floundering in your faith because you feel insignificant, there's help for you. Christian counselor Dr. Minnie Claiborne has written a powerful prescription for permanent healing of emotional hurts and pain and offers wisdom for freedom from mental oppression and anguish. In eight short chapters, Dr. Claiborne connects you to the Father's love where you will find healing and emotional wholeness. For more information and resources, visit drminnie.net.

HOW TO SAY IT

Aramaic. air-ah-**MAY**-ik.

Gethsemane. geth-**SEH**-muh-nee.

PREPARE FOR NEXT SUNDAY

Read **Luke 2:36-38; Acts 2:16-21, 21:8-9** and next week's lesson, "Prophesying Daughters."

DAILY HOME BIBLE READINGS

MONDAY
Prayer for Peter in Prison
(Acts 12:5–11)

TUESDAY
Pray for a Successful Ministry
(Romans 15:22–33)

WEDNESDAY
Pray for Inner Strength and Power
(Ephesians 3:14–21)

THURSDAY
Pray the Prayer of Our Lord
(Matthew 6:7–13)

FRIDAY
Pray for Your Abusers
(Luke 6:22–33)

SATURDAY
Pray to Avoid Trials
(Luke 22:39–46)

SUNDAY
Jesus Prays for His Disciples
(John 17:13–24)

Sources:

Abraham, Kenneth A. *The Matthew Henry Study Bible, King James Version.* Dallas, TX: World Bible Publishers, 1994. 2155–2158.

Brown, Raymond Edward. *The Gospel According to John Xiii–Xxi: A New Introduction and Commentary.* Garden City, NY: Doubleday, 1966.

Bruce, F. F. *The Gospel of John: Introduction, Exposition and Notes.* Grand Rapids, MI: Wm. B. Eerdmans, 1983.

Carson, D. A. *The Farewell Discourse and Final Prayer of Jesus: An Exposition of John 14–17.* Grand Rapids, MI: Baker Book House, 1980. 173–207.

Claiborne, Minnie. *Prayer Therapy: Stop Hurting.* Ministry in Art Publishing, 2006. www.drminnie.net

Meyer, F. B. *Gospel of John: The Life and Light of Man, Love to the Uttermost.* Fort Washington, PA: Christian Literature Crusade, 1988.

Morris, Leon. *The Gospel According to John: The English Text with Introduction, Exposition and Notes.* Grand Rapids, MI: Eerdmans, 1971. 716-738.

Unger, Merrill. *Unger's Bible Dictionary.* Chicago, IL: Moody Press, 1981. 596.

Zodhiates, Spiros, Baker, Warren. eds. *Hebrew Greek Key Word Study Bible, King James Version.* 2nd ed. Chattanooga, TN: AMG Publishers, 1991. 1709, 1717.

PROPHESYING DAUGHTERS

BIBLE BASIS: Luke 2:36–38; Acts 2:16–21, 21:8–9

BIBLE TRUTH: Women are used by God to speak for God.

MEMORY VERSE: "And it shall come to pass in the last days, saith God, I will pour out of my Spirit upon all flesh: and your sons and your daughters shall prophesy, and your young men shall see visions, and your old men shall dream dreams" (Acts 2:17, KJV).

LESSON AIM: By the end of this lesson, we will REVIEW how God called and empowered women to proclaim His message, AFFIRM contributions of godly women to the Church's mission, and ADVOCATE for greater recognition of God-called women in the Church.

BACKGROUND SCRIPTURES: Luke 2:36–38; Acts 1:12–14, 2:16–21, 21:8–9— Read and incorporate the insights gained from the Background Scriptures into your study of the lesson.

TEACHER PREPARATION

MATERIALS NEEDED: Bibles (several different versions), Quarterly Commentary/Teacher Manual, Adult Quarterly, teaching resources such as charts, worksheets/handouts, paper, pens, pencils

OTHER MATERIALS NEEDED / TEACHER'S NOTES:

_____

_____

LESSON OVERVIEW

LIFE NEED FOR TODAY'S LESSON
All people have a unique purpose in life. How do we affirm each individual's purpose? The Gospel of Luke and the Book of Acts provide examples of women responding to God's call.

BIBLE LEARNING
The prophetess, Anna, and Philips' four prophetess daughters are some examples that God pours out His Spirit on women.

BIBLE APPLICATION
The pouring out of God's Spirit on men and women at Pentecost is the fulfillment of God's promise in Joel 2:28–29.

STUDENTS' RESPONSES
Believers express joy that Joel's prophecy affirms women.

LESSON SCRIPTURE

LUKE 2:36–38; ACTS 2:16–21, 21:8–9, KJV

Luke **2:36** And there was one Anna, a prophetess, the daughter of Phanuel, of the tribe of Aser: she was of a great age, and had lived with an husband seven years from her virginity;

37 And she was a widow of about fourscore and four years, which departed not from the temple, but served God with fastings and prayers night and day.

38 And she coming in that instant gave thanks likewise unto the Lord, and spake of him to all them that looked for redemption in Jerusalem.

Acts 2:16 But this is that which was spoken by the prophet Joel;

17 And it shall come to pass in the last days, saith God, I will pour out of my Spirit upon all flesh: and your sons and your daughters shall prophesy, and your young men shall see visions, and your old men shall dream dreams:

18 And on my servants and on my handmaidens I will pour out in those days of my Spirit; and they shall prophesy:

19 And I will shew wonders in heaven above, and signs in the earth beneath; blood, and fire, and vapour of smoke:

20 The sun shall be turned into darkness, and the moon into blood, before the great and notable day of the Lord come:

21 And it shall come to pass, that whosoever shall call on the name of the Lord shall be saved.

21:8 And the next day we that were of Paul's company departed, and came unto Caesarea: and we entered into the house of Philip the evangelist, which was one of the seven; and abode with him.

9 And the same man had four daughters, virgins, which did prophesy.

BIBLICAL DEFINITIONS

A. Redemption (**Luke 2:38**) *lutrosis* (Gk.)— Ransoming, deliverance

B. Pour out (**Acts 2:17**) *echeo* (Gk.)—To pour forth, bestow, gush, run greedily out, shed abroad, spill

LIGHT ON THE WORD

Upper Room Women. Jesus instructed His followers to go to Jerusalem and wait for the coming of the Holy Ghost. They obeyed, and 120 men and women assembled. The Scripture clearly states that this number includes certain women: Mary, the mother of Jesus, who was mentioned by name, was present (**Acts 1:14**) along with the Apostles' wives (cf. **1 Corinthians 9:5**). Throughout Jesus' ministry, female followers were devoted to His work (**Luke 8:2–3**). Women were also filled with the Holy Ghost, just as the prophet Joel prophesied (**Acts 2:17**).

Pentecost. Celebrated fifty days after Passover, Pentecost was also called the "Feast of Harvest" and the "Feast of First Fruits" (**Leviticus 23:5–21**). Pentecost is also celebrated as Shavuot or the Feast of Weeks, which celebrates Moses receiving the Ten Commandments on Mount Sinai. Christians celebrate Pentecost to commemorate the outpouring of the gifts of the Holy Spirit and speaking in tongues. While Shavuot also represents the Jews being freed from slavery to Egypt, Pentecost represents humankind being freed from slavery to sin.

TEACHING THE BIBLE LESSON

LIFE NEED FOR TODAY'S LESSON

AIM: Students will agree that God also uses women to speak to His people.

INTRODUCTION

Women Who Prophesy

Throughout the Bible, women have been used by God to prophesy—to speak to God's people. Miriam (**Exodus 15:20**), Deborah (**Judges 4:4**), Huldah (**2 Kings 22:14**), Noadiah (**Nehemiah 6:14**), and a woman identified as "the prophetess" (**Isaiah 8:3**) guided God's people in the Old Testament. In the New Testament, Anna (**Luke 2:38**), and Phillip's four daughters (**Acts 21:9**) are recognized as prophetesses.

The prophet Joel prophesied that God would pour out His Spirit on everyone—women included—and He did! The power of God's Spirit equips men and women to fulfill Christ's mission (**Ephesians 1:13–14**).

BIBLE LEARNING

AIM: Students will affirm the bibical truth that women speak for God.

I. A WOMAN DECLARES THE MESSIAH (LUKE 2:36-38)

The **Gospel of Luke** highlights a prophetess named Anna, from the Israelite tribe of Asher. Anna was a widow who devoted her life to God. She prayed, fasted, and served in Jerusalem and "departed not from the temple" (**v. 37**).

Anna longed to see the Messiah face-to-face. God granted her heart's desire when Mary and Joseph walked into the Temple with the baby Jesus. Anna immediately praised and thanked God for allowing her to see Jesus and witness the unfolding of the messianic prophecies. Inspired by the Holy Spirit, Anna spoke boldly declaring the baby Jesus is the promised one bringing salvation and redemption.

36 And there was one Anna, a prophetess, the daughter of Phanuel, of the tribe of Aser: she was of a great age, and had lived with an husband seven years from her virginity; 37 And she was a widow of about fourscore and four years, which departed not from the temple, but served God with fastings and prayers night and day. 38 And she coming in that instant gave thanks likewise unto the Lord, and spake of him to all them that looked for redemption in Jerusalem.

Anna's name means grace or gracious. The daughter of Phanuel, Anna, was from the tribe of Asher, who were descendants of Israel's tenth son (**Genesis 30:13**). She was a holy servant of God dedicated to fasting, prayer, and serving in the Temple. Anna, who had been waiting to see the Messiah, gives thanks, announcing to everyone that the Messiah is bringing redemption (Gk. *lutrosis*, **LOO-troh-sees**).

SEARCH THE SCRIPTURES

QUESTION 1

Why does the Gospel writer, Luke, include the prophetess Anna in accounting the events surrounding the Messiah's birth?

Luke recognizes God's faithfulness to Anna.

QUESTION 2

Why is it important to affirm that God also speaks through women?

God still uses women today.

LIGHT ON THE WORD

Anna Announces the Redeemer

Anna announces to everyone who wants to listen that Jesus is the redeemer! Mary and

Joseph brought Jesus to the Temple to fulfill the law of the mother's purification after childbirth and redeeming the firstborn (**Exodus 13:2**; **Numbers 8:17**; **18:14–16**; **Leviticus 12:1–8**). The Greek translation of the Old Testament even uses this same root (*lutroo*) when giving the instructions for this rite (**Exodus 13:13**). This baby, redeemed with a sacrifice of two doves, will be the one to redeem all humanity from sin. Hallelujah!

II. WOMEN ARE FILLED (ACTS 2:16-21)

On the Day of Pentecost, Peter addressed the crowd in Jerusalem who marvel at hearing men and women speak in other tongues or in their languages. Peter explains that this occurrence is the partial fulfillment of Joel's prophecy (**Joel 2:28-29**). Christians are now God's temple, the dwelling place of the Holy Spirit (**1 Corinthians 3:16**). People from all nations, cultures, and groups, regardless of gender, race, or social status, can be filled with the Holy Spirit, empowered to speak God's words—both young and old, men and women.

Acts 2:16 But this is that which was spoken by the prophet Joel; 17 And it shall come to pass in the last days, saith God, I will pour out of my Spirit upon all flesh: and your sons and your daughters shall prophesy, and your young men shall see visions, and your old men shall dream dreams:

"In the last days" is often used in the Old Testament to mean "in a future time" and appears in several Scriptures (**Genesis 49:1**; **Isaiah 2:2**; **Micah 3:1**). A critical time for the Jews is the time of the Messiah's reign, which is anticipated as a glorious time to live under the Messiah's rulership.

"To prophesy" (Gk. *propheteuo*, **pro-feh-TEW-oh**) has several different meanings. In **Matthew**, it means foretelling the future. In **Luke**, to prophesy is to celebrate the praises of God. In both, to prophesy is to be under divine influence, whether telling the future, celebrating the praises of God, giving instruction in the duties of religious purposes, or even speaking in foreign languages or tongues.

In former times, the will of God was communicated to the prophets by visions and dreams through prophets called seers (**1 Samuel 9:9**). God informed Abimelech in a dream that Sarah was the wife of Abraham (**Genesis 20:3**). God will continue to speak to His people through visions and dreams.

18 And on my servants and on my handmaidens I will pour out in those days of my Spirit; and they shall prophesy:

In Scripture, the worshipers of God were often referred to as servants of God. Therefore, God chooses on whom He will pour His Spirit. God is the One to give to His servants and handmaidens the gift of prophecy—proclaiming that God's Son came into the world to save the lost.

19 And I will shew wonders in heaven above, and signs in the earth beneath; blood, and fire, and vapour of smoke: 20 The sun shall be turned into darkness, and the moon into blood, before that great and notable day of the Lord come:

The "day of the Lord" represents any day God manifests Himself, but in particular, when He will pass judgment or punish wrongdoers. God is good and just. But for those who reject the Lord, judgment day is frightful. The fire and smoke also remind us of Sinai, when the presence of God was with the people. The "vapour of smoke" means a column or shaft of smoke that is here for a moment and then disappears (cf **James 4:14**).

21 And it shall come to pass, that whosoever shall call on the name of the Lord shall be saved.

There is only one way to avoid the prophesied judgment—sincerely call on the name of the Lord. The last days include the days of great salvation. Throughout the last days, sinners can be saved by calling on the name of the Lord. Those who recognize their need to be saved, who believe that Jesus is risen from the dead, and who receive Jesus as Lord and Savior will be saved (**Romans 10:9-10, 13**).

SEARCH THE SCRIPTURES

QUESTION 3
Why is it significant that Joel's prophesy explicitly mentions women?

Women are in God's plan to be used by Him. Answers will vary.

QUESTION 4
Who will be able to escape judgment?

Those who call on the name of the Lord and are saved will escape judgment.

LIGHT ON THE WORD

The Spirit Poured Out
God freely promises to pour out His Spirit to refresh or renew and purify or sanctify the soul. To "pour out" means to be given out in vast amounts, as in pouring from a fountain that has no barriers, hindrances, or restrictions. The "Spirit" in this passage is the Holy Spirit, the third person of the Trinity. The gifts of the Spirit flow from the Holy Spirit (**1 Corinthians 4-10**). He, the Holy Spirit, will refresh, renew, purify, and sanctify the receiving soul.

Women and men alike are recipients of God's Spirit. Never should a female question her ability to be used by God. But know, too, that God is a God of order.

III. WOMEN PROPHESY (ACTS 21:8-9)
Philip was one of the first seven deacons (**Acts 6:1-6**) who witnessed to an Ethiopian eunuch and Philip's daughters were unmarried "virgins" (Gk. *parthenos*, **par-THEH-noce**), which might also mean unmarried teenagers. The notation that they were unmarried indicates a conscious decision to remain devoted only to the Lord (cf. **1 Corinthians 7:34**). The Scripture offers no extensive details about these four prophetesses. They are unnamed, and all that is recorded about their specific involvement in ministry is that they prophesied.

21:8 And the next day we that were of Paul's company departed, and came unto Caesarea: and we entered into the house of Philip the evangelist, which was one of the seven; and abode with him. 9 And the same man had four daughters, virgins, which did prophesy.

Paul and others in his group experienced the prophetic ministry of Philip's daughters. Even though their mother, Philip's wife, isn't mentioned, she may have been present. Philip was raising his family in the fear of the Lord; his children were serving and trusting God. His four daughters are gifted explicitly by the Holy Spirit to prophesy.

SEARCH THE SCRIPTURES

QUESTION 5

Provide reasons that Philip's daughters were respected and their prophecies valued.

Philip raised his daughters in the fear of the Lord. They served with reverence and respect.

QUESTION 6

What do we learn about women's roles in the Church today?

Answers will vary.

LIGHT ON THE WORD

Family Witness

Philip's witness began at home. His children learned to love Jesus because Philip loved Jesus. Philip was used by God to minister to the Ethiopian eunuch, who is credited with bringing the Gospel to Ethiopia (**Acts 8:26–40**). Imagine Philip's excitement in relating this experience to his daughters! And imagine the daughter's passionate desire to follow Jesus just like dad. As is often seen today, when parents love the Lord and are involved in ministry, their private and public witness encourages their children to follow in their footsteps.

BIBLE APPLICATION

AIM: Students will identify ways that women serve in the ministry today.

There are many opportunities to prophesy and share the Good News other than ministering behind a podium. Teaching, evangelizing, writing, singing, fostering/adopting children, visiting the sick and helping seniors, interceding, feeding the homeless, mentoring young women, ministering to women prisoners and those released from prison, encouraging girls and women rescued from sex-trafficking, cooking, counseling the discouraged—and the list goes on—are examples of ways women are serving in the church today. What would you add to this list?

STUDENTS' RESPONSES

AIM: Students will encourage one another to do the work of the ministry.

Both women and men are God's mouthpiece. And we are His hands and feet. God calls us to minister to a dying world by meeting the needs of men and women, boys and girls in our families, churches, and communities. What will God have you do today?

PRAYER

Father, we love studying Your Word! Thank You for this lesson that highlights Your love for everyone. And thank You for focusing the spotlight on women who were devoted servants to You. May we follow their lead and serve You with complete and total devotion. In the Name of Jesus, we pray. Amen.

DIG A LITTLE DEEPER

Luke's Gospel highlights women more than any other Gospel. This Apostle's biblical accounts demonstrate women's spiritual strength and sensitivity to the Holy Spirit, which elevates women from the patriarchal limitations of their day. In the first chapters of his book, the author contrasts Elizabeth's faith as she responds to the angel Gabriel's announcement that she will have a child in her old age, with the doubt of her husband, Zacharias, who is chastened and unable to speak until John's birth (**Luke 1:5–25; 57–80**). Luke echoes the Virgin Mary's knowledge of

Scripture as she sings the Magnificat—her song of praise (**Luke 1:46–55**). And rather than overlooking Anna, Luke respects her title as a prophetess and publicizes God's reward of this widow's faithfulness. In seeing the baby, Jesus, Anna's hope is realized, and she spreads the news of redemption in Jerusalem.

As a physician, Luke documents Jesus' healing of Peter's mother-in-law (**Luke 4:38–39**), the interruption of the funeral procession when Jesus raised the widow of Nain's son (**Luke 7:11**), the little girl whom Jesus awoke from her eternal sleep (**Luke 51–52**), and the woman with the issue of blood who pressed through the crowds to touch the tassels of Jesus' garment (**Luke 8:43–48**). Luke's empathy for women—Mary Magdalene, who was demon-possessed (**Luke 8:2**) and the infirm woman who could not stand up straight (**Luke 13:10–17**)—mirrors Jesus, who delivered Mary and straightened the bent woman. Luke reveals the love of the uninvited guest at Simon's home who wiped Jesus' feet with her hair (**Luke 7:36–50**). Also, Luke notes that women were the financial supporters of Jesus' itinerant ministry (**Luke 8:3**).

We learn that Jesus' mother was worried about her Son, so much so that she took Jesus' brothers to help bring Jesus home (**Luke 8:19–21**). And, we overhear Martha's and Mary's dispute between serving Jesus and sitting at His feet (**Luke 10:38–42**). A persistent widow teaches us how to be steadfast in prayer (**Luke 18:1**), and a widow's offering of two mites teaches us about sacrificial giving (**Luke 21:1–4**).

Luke records that the women—Mary Magdalene, Joanna, Mary the mother of James "and the other women with them"—were the last at the Cross and the first at the tomb (**Luke 23:49; 55–56; 24:1–10**). And Luke pens the first preaching of the Good

News that Jesus is risen through the words of those whom God chose—the women (**Luke 24:10, 12**).

In her exceptional book, author Ruth Tucker does an extraordinary review of the women of the New Testament from which this summary is derived. It's one resource every woman may want to include in her library. Please see the reference in the Sources list.

HOW TO SAY IT

Phanuel. FAH-noo-ell.

Azotus. AH-zoe-tuss.

Caesarea. KYE-sare-EE-uh.

PREPARE FOR NEXT SUNDAY

Read **John 4:25-42** and next week's lesson, "Called to Evangelize."

Sources:
Acts. The Preacher's Outline and Sermon Bible. Leadership Ministries Worldwide. Chattanooga, TN: Alpha-Omega Ministries, 2003.
Barnes, Albert. *Barnes' Notes on the New Testament.* Grand Rapids, MI: Kregel Publications, 1962.
Black, Mark C. *Luke.* The College Press NIV Commentary. Joplin, MO: College Press Publishing Company, 1996.
Carson, D.A., Walter W. Wessel, and Walter L. Liefeld. *Matthew, Mark, Luke.* The Expositor's Bible Commentary. Vol. 8. Frank E. Gaebelein, general editor. Grand Rapids, MI: Zondervan, 1984.
Henry, Matthew. *Matthew Henry's Commentary on the Whole Bible: New Modern Edition.* Vols. 1-6. Peabody, MA: Hendrickson Publishers, Inc., 2009.
Keener, Craig S. *The IVP Bible Background Commentary: New Testament.* Downers Grove, IL: InterVarsity Press, 1994.
Pfeiffer, Charles F., Howard F. Vos, John Rea, eds. *Wycliffe Bible Dictionary.* Peabody, MA: Hendrickson Publishers, Inc., 1998.
Strong, James. *The New Strong's Exhaustive Concordance of the Bible.* Nashville, TN: Thomas Nelson, 2003.
Thayer, Joseph Henry. *A Greek-English Lexicon of the New Testament.* New York: American Book Company, 1889.
Tucker, Ruth A. *Daughters of the Church: Women and Ministry From New Testament Times to the Present.* Grand Rapids, Michigan: Zondervan. 1987. 49-51.Vine, W.E. *Vine's Complete Expository Dictionary of Old and New Testament Words.* Nashville, TN: Thomas Nelson, 1996.
Walvoord, John F. and Roy B. Zuck. *The Bible Knowledge Commentary: An Exposition of the Scriptures.* New Testament. Wheaton, IL: Victor Books, 1983.

DAILY HOME BIBLE READINGS

MONDAY
Jesus Supports Mary's Choice
(Luke 10:38–42)

TUESDAY
Jesus Responds to Sister's Call
(John 11:1–11)

WEDNESDAY
Jesus Raises Lazarus; Mary Believes
(John 11:38–45)

THURSDAY
Women Carry Resurrection
Message to Apostles
(Luke 24:5–10)

FRIDAY
Jesus' Final Words and Ascension
(Luke 24:44–53)

SATURDAY
Simeon Sees Impact of
Jesus' Ministry
(Luke 2:28-35)

SUNDAY
The Spirit Empowers
Daughters to Prophesy
(Luke 2:36-38; Acts 2:16-21; 21:8-9)

COMMENTS / NOTES:

CALLED TO EVANGELIZE

BIBLE BASIS: JOHN 4:25-42

BIBLE TRUTH: After meeting Jesus, the Samaritan woman becomes an evangelist.

MEMORY VERSE: "And many of the Samaritans of that city believed on him for the saying of the woman, which testified, He told me all that ever I did" (John 4:39, KJV)

LESSON AIM: By the end of this lesson, we will ANALYZE the barriers Jesus crossed in speaking with the Samaritan woman, SENSE the wonder the Samaritan woman felt in her meeting with Jesus, and SHARE with others the transforming power of God at work in their lives.

BACKGROUND SCRIPTURES: John 1:37-51, 4:25-42 —Read and incorporate the insights gained from the Background Scriptures into your study of the lesson.

TEACHER PREPARATION

MATERIALS NEEDED: Bibles (several different versions), Quarterly Commentary/Teacher Manual, Adult Quarterly, teaching resources such as charts, worksheets/handouts, paper, pens, pencils

OTHER MATERIALS NEEDED / TEACHER'S NOTES:

_____

_____

LESSON OVERVIEW

LIFE NEED FOR TODAY'S LESSON
Some people wonder if they are good enough to give direction to others. What is the best way to share our witness? The woman at the well was considered an outcast, but after meeting Jesus, she eagerly became a witness and brought others to Jesus.

BIBLE LEARNING
Jesus changes a woman's life, and that woman changes her community.

BIBLE APPLICATION
Believers are convinced that no one is too much of an outcast of society that Jesus cannot reach them and make their lives new.

STUDENTS' RESPONSES
Believers spread the Gospel of Jesus Christ.

LESSON SCRIPTURE

JOHN 4:25-42, KJV

25 The woman saith unto him, I know that Messias cometh, which is called Christ: when he is come, he will tell us all things.

26 Jesus saith unto her, I that speak unto thee am he.

27 And upon this came his disciples, and marvelled that he talked with the woman: yet no man said, What seekest thou? or, Why talkest thou with her?

28 The woman then left her waterpot, and went her way into the city, and saith to the men,

29 Come, see a man, which told me all things that ever I did: is not this the Christ?

30 Then they went out of the city, and came unto him.

31 In the mean while his disciples prayed him, saying, Master, eat.

32 But he said unto them, I have meat to eat that ye know not of.

33 Therefore said the disciples one to another, Hath any man brought him ought to eat?

34 Jesus saith unto them, My meat is to do the will of him that sent me, and to finish his work.

35 Say not ye, There are yet four months, and then cometh harvest? behold, I say unto you, Lift up your eyes, and look on the fields; for they are white already to harvest.

36 And he that reapeth receiveth wages, and gathereth fruit unto life eternal: that both he that soweth and he that reapeth may rejoice together.

37 And herein is that saying true, One soweth, and another reapeth.

38 I sent you to reap that whereon ye bestowed no labour: other men laboured, and ye are entered into their labours.

39 And many of the Samaritans of that city believed on him for the saying of the woman, which testified, He told me all that ever I did.

40 So when the Samaritans were come unto him, they besought him that he would tarry with them: and he abode there two days.

41 And many more believed because of his own word;

42 And said unto the woman, Now we believe, not because of thy saying: for we have heard him ourselves, and know that this is indeed the Christ, the Saviour of the world.

BIBLICAL DEFINITIONS

A. Marvelled (John 4:27) *thaumazo* (Gk.)— To wonder or admire

B. Testified (v. 39) *martureo* (Gk.)—To be an earnest witness, telling the truth about what is known

LIGHT ON THE WORD

Jacob's Well. Today there is a well near Sychar, which Samaritans believed was built by Jacob. A narrow opening four feet long led from the floor of the vault into the well, which was dug through limestone. The ground mentioned by John had been purchased by Jacob (**Genesis 33:19**). The area was later wrested by force from the Amorites (**Genesis 38:22**). The well is near the base of Mount Gerizim, which was as holy to the Samaritans as Mt. Zion was to the Jews. Many religious differences like this led to disdain between Jews and Samaritans.

The Woman at the Well. The Samaritan woman approaches to draw water from the well at the heat of the day, which is noontime. Most women are at the well during the cool hours of the morning, which is also their time to socialize. The Samaritan woman, who is not explicitly named, has had five husbands and is currently living with a sixth man. She may have been divorced or widowed several times, but now she is living with someone else's husband, which explains why she draws water in the heat of the day. She probably wants to avoid the other women's judging eyes and gossiping whispers.

TEACHING THE BIBLE LESSON

LIFE NEED FOR TODAY'S LESSON

AIM: Students will explore the conflict between Jews and Samaritans.

INTRODUCTION

Samaritans

In **John 4**, Jesus and His disciples left Judea to return to Galilee. The route led them directly through Samaria. Although Jews and Samaritans both descended from ancient Israel, their religious practices and beliefs were slightly different, and there was long-standing hostility between them. When Jesus' disciples went into the city to buy food, Jesus rested by the well in the heat of the day. As Jesus rested, a Samaritan woman approached the well to draw water. Because of social customs where men didn't speak to women in public, the woman did not expect Jesus to say anything to her. But Jesus asks her to draw water for Him and promises that He could give her living or spiritual water. There at the well, they have a theological debate. As the conversation progresses, the Samaritan woman realizes that Jesus is no ordinary Jewish man. Just

before the disciples returned, Jesus revealed that He is Israel's long-awaited Messiah.

BIBLE LEARNING

AIM: Students review the origin of the name of God.

I. "I AM" (JOHN 4:25-30)

A common phrase Jesus uses in the Gospel of John is "I am He." The phrase reveals Jesus to be the great "I Am," which is God's name (Exodus 3:14). Although Jesus' disciples struggle throughout the **Gospel of John** to understand that Jesus is the Messiah, the Samaritan woman does not. When the disciples return from the city, the woman leaves her water jug at the well and runs to tell the good news of the Man who "told her everything [she] had ever done." Although the disciples were surprised to find Jesus speaking publicly with a Samaritan woman, they kept their thoughts to themselves. The woman ran and told everyone in the city about her encounter with Jesus, and the Samaritans went out to meet Him.

25 The woman saith unto him, I know that Messias cometh, which is called Christ: when he is come, he will tell us all things. 26 Jesus saith unto her, I that speak unto thee am he.

While the Jews and the Samaritans both worshiped the same God, their understanding of the Word of God was very different. The Samaritan Scriptures only included the Pentateuch—the first five books of the Old Testament. Their religious tradition rejected the writings of the prophets. Also, they believed that Mt. Gerizim was the true place of worship, not Mt. Zion and Jerusalem, which is the traditional place of worship for the

Jews. The Samaritans recognized that the Messiah would come; they expected Him to be a teacher who would reveal all truth (**Deuteronomy 18:15-20**).

The conversation between Jesus and the Samaritan woman both challenged and clarified her understanding of the Messiah. When the woman explained her view (which was the Samaritan view) of the Messiah, Jesus confessed that He was the Christ, the very One she had anticipated. His revelation was the summation of their systematic and theological conversation. Jesus' announcement that He was the Messiah is especially notable because this is the first time Jesus openly stated who He was. Prior to Jesus's trial, Jesus did not profess to the Jews that He was the Messiah. But Jesus revealed the truth of God to a woman at the well.

27 And upon this came his disciples, and marvelled that he talked with the woman: yet no man said, What seekest thou? or, Why talkest thou with her?

The disciples had left Jesus at the well and were surprised to find him talking to the woman when they returned. This was a violation of several customs. It was rare for a Jewish teacher to engage a woman in public discourse. The Jews saw the Samaritans as unclean, so there was animosity between the two cultures. It was a violation of Jewish laws of purification to eat or drink anything belonging to or coming from the Samaritans.

When the disciples returned, they "marvelled" (Gk. *thaumazo*, **thow-MOD-zo**) or wondered why He was having a conversation with the Samaritan woman. The word implies that this was a miracle or

very unusual, but the disciples respected Jesus too much to question His behavior.

28 The woman then left her waterpot, and went her way into the city, and saith to the men, 29 Come, see a man, which told me all things that ever I did: is not this the Christ? 30 Then they went out of the city, and came unto him.

While some speculate that the disciples' return interrupted the woman's conversation with Jesus, it is more likely that the discussion had ended. The woman made her way back to Sychar to tell what happened to her at the well. She was so excited that she left her waterpot. She had come to the well to get water but hurried back to the city without it, because she had a more important task. This stranger who knew all about her past was not just an ordinary man. He was an extraordinary man, the declared Messiah, who had such a profound impact on her that she ran to tell the men of the town—the teachers and leaders who would appreciate a theological discussion with Jesus.

SEARCH THE SCRIPTURES

QUESTION 1
Why was the Samaritan woman so responsive to the fact that Jesus was the Messiah?

The encounter with Jesus changed her life. Answers will vary.

QUESTION 2
Have you ever had a life-altering spiritual experience at an unexpected time or in an unexpected place?

Answers will vary.

LIGHT ON THE WORD

Needing Jesus

Jesus confronted the Samaritan woman with the reality of her life, a reality with which she was painfully aware. Rejected by the respectable women, this wounded spirit—either a victim or a convenient distraction—had finally come to terms with her need (**4:15**), her sin (**4:19**), and her condition (**4:26**). To quench her spiritual thirst, Jesus gave her living water.

The fact that she was a woman, particularly a woman with a stained reputation, meant that the elders of Sychar would not accept any theological or religious information from her. But the woman's plea was so sincere that the Samaritans listened and left the city to find Jesus. They wanted to see Jesus for themselves because of her urgent invitation.

II. I HAVE (vv. 31-38)

While the woman was in the city sharing her testimony, the disciples encouraged Jesus to eat, but He gave them an unexpected response. The disciples were as puzzled as was the woman to whom Jesus offered living water. Jesus told the disciples that they did not know about His food.

Mirroring the woman's confusion, the disciples wondered who might have brought Jesus something to eat. However, Jesus explained that His "food" was the work God sent Him to do because the fields were ripe for harvesting.

31 In the mean while his disciples prayed him, saying, Master, eat. 32 But he said unto them, I have meat to eat that ye know not of. 33 Therefore said the disciples one to another, Hath any man brought him ought to eat?

While the Samaritans were on their way, Jesus spoke privately with His disciples who had returned to the well. John records the conversation in **verses 31-38**. The disciples went to buy food from town and were concerned because Jesus had not eaten. They knew He should have been hungry. When Jesus rejected the food, they did not understand. Jesus' words were confusing.

Ancient teachers sometimes used physical food as a figure of speech for spiritual nourishment. The disciples thought that when Jesus used the word "meat" (Gk. *brosis*, **BRO-sees**), He had already eaten. The term "meat" usually refers to natural food of any kind, and when used metaphorically, the meaning is made clear (cf **1 Corinthians 10:3**). But the disciples were baffled. Why wasn't Jesus hungry?

34 Jesus saith unto them, My meat is to do the will of him that sent me, and to finish his work.

Jesus' explained that He is sustained by doing His Father's will. He told them that when He does His Father's will, He is satisfied much like their bodies are satisfied when they eat. In this case, His meat was the truth-encounter with the woman that changed her life. Also, Jesus wanted to reach the Samaritans. Jesus was satisfied because He was doing the work of His Father. Jesus made a bold statement to say He was being fed by doing what His Father told Him to do.

35 Say not ye, There are yet four months, and then cometh harvest? behold, I say unto you, Lift up your eyes, and look on the fields; for they are white already to harvest.

Jesus refers to the four months between planting and harvesting. In March, the barley fields turn white; they are ready for harvest. Jesus was concerned about the souls of the people, the lost souls He had come to save (**Luke 19:10**). He was changing the focus of their attention from a worldly perspective to a spiritual one. In essence, Jesus wanted them to see with spiritual eyes rather than with natural eyes.

36 And he that reapeth receiveth wages, and gathereth fruit unto life eternal: that both he that soweth and he that reapeth may rejoice together. 37 And herein is that saying true, One soweth, and another reapeth. 38 I sent you to reap that whereon ye bestowed no labour: other men laboured, and ye are entered into their labours.

In a natural harvest, the person who reaps may be one person, while the person who sows may be another person. Many people work in the field before the actual harvest. Harvesting is a team effort, although the team members may not work at the same time. It was important for the disciples to understand the principle of uniting sowers and reapers.

In **verse 37**, Jesus explains an ancient truism regarding sowers and reapers. Jesus wanted them to see with their spiritual eyes. The Old Testament prophets had put in the work, doing their part to prepare the soil. The last in their tradition was John the Baptist. Christ also wanted the disciples to understand that this work would continue.

Paul uses this same metaphor when speaking to the Corinthian church: "I have planted, Apollos watered; but God gave the increase" (**1 Corinthians 3:6**). God is the key component. He is the One that causes growth. Each person plays an active role, but there is only one purpose.

SEARCH THE SCRIPTURES

QUESTION 3
Why are the metaphors of water and food helpful in describing spiritual needs?

We all need water and food to survive. Satisfying spiritual thirst and hunger is essential to growing spiritually.

QUESTION 4
When was the last time you let someone know about God's indescribable love?

Answers will vary.

LIGHT ON THE WORD
The Father's Work
It was imperative that Jesus accomplish His Father's work. Isn't this our passion, too? For the child of God, doing the will of the Father is a source of our strength and satisfaction. It's our purpose. As believers, we should periodically examine ourselves to determine whether we are truly doing the will of God.

Jesus was hungry to see people saved. Do we have that same hunger to see people come to Jesus? Are we willing to push past our comfort zone to minister to others? Are we ready to go to the least likely places when we would rather go home? Is Christ's passion our passion? What impact could your testimony have on the people around you?

III. I BELIEVE (vv. 39-42)

The Samaritan woman's testimony was simple. She believed that Jesus was the Messiah because He had told her everything she had ever done. The woman believed in Jesus because Jesus saw her. For the Samaritans, her honest and straightforward testimony inspired their curiosity and belief, and they invited Jesus to stay.

When others heard Jesus for themselves, they believed. They told the woman that they believe, not because of what she said, but because they had a personal encounter with Him.

39 And many of the Samaritans of that city believed on him for the saying of the woman, which testified, He told me all that ever I did. 40 So when the Samaritans were come unto him, they besought him that he would tarry with them: and he abode there two days. 41 And many more believed because of his own word; 42 And said unto the woman, Now we believe, not because of thy saying: for we have heard him ourselves, and know that this is indeed the Christ, the Saviour of the world.

The Samaritans of the city of Sychar listened to the woman's testimony. Jesus had talked to her. He knew all about her sin, her lies, and her secrets. The men of the town recognized her, but something was different. Her encounter with Jesus changed her. They saw Jesus and believed for themselves.

The woman "testified" (Gk. *martureo*, **mar-too-REH-oh**); she was an earnest witness. Witnesses simply tell the truth about what they know. As a result, these men's interest was sparked, and they ecided to go to the source. At the well, they found Jesus. Now they desired more. They wanted Jesus to remain in their city, and He did for two days.

SEARCH THE SCRIPTURES

QUESTION 5
Why is our testimony such a powerful witnessing tool? Why are we sometimes reluctant to tell the truth about ourselves by sharing our testimony?

Answers will vary.

QUESTION 6
Will you walk with a friend, neighbor, or family member to lead them to a personal encounter with Jesus?
Answers will vary.

LIGHT ON THE WORD
The Power of Testimony
Testimony is a powerful witnessing tool. The Samaritans believed because of the woman's testimony. Today, we believe because of the eyewitnesses in the New Testament and the "testimonies" throughout the entire Bible. The Samaritans heard what the woman said. We read and "hear" what the Scriptures say. The Samaritans saw her transformation. We see the transformation of the biblical characters throughout the pages of God's Word. The Samaritans knew who she was and saw who she became because of this Man, Jesus.

Our testimony is also powerful. When people see our actions and "read" our lives, it's a witness. When people listen to how we speak, it should lead them to personal faith. The transformation of our lives should be proof that Christ Jesus is the Messiah! Our testimony should make our family, friends, and acquaintances want to know more about Jesus. They will find Him when they seek Him with their whole heart.

BIBLE APPLICATION
AIM: Students will be willing to cross cultural barriers to share their testimony.

Globally, ethnic and cultural groups struggle to relate to each other. Cultural misunderstandings may lead to violence, including the abuse of women and children.

This passage points us to an alternative model for living. It encourages us to build relationships even when cultural norms discourage us from doing so. It reminds us that as followers of Jesus Christ, we model His sacrificial love, grace, and mercy to everyone we meet.

STUDENTS' RESPONSES

AIM: Students will tell the Good News!

Go tell the Good News of Jesus Christ! You never know who might be transformed by your testimony. Share what God has done in your life with your family and friends and also in your community as God gives opportunity. Explore the possibility of interfaith or interracial dialogue. The church is the hands and feet of Jesus in the world. Let's pursue every opportunity to love others as freely as Jesus loves us.

PRAYER

Father, Jesus went out of His way to minister to the Samaritan woman. What an example that He came to seek and save the lost! Thank you for finding us, for drawing us to you through the testimony and witness of others. Help us, Holy Spirit, to be powerful participants in sharing the Good News of Jesus Christ. In His Name, we pray. Amen.

DIG A LITTLE DEEPER

The work of evangelism involves the ability to share your testimony. Do you know how to share your testimony if you only have 3 minutes to do so? Do you know how to share your testimony in 30 minutes or an hour?

Outline your testimony with a beginning, middle, and end. Now, write it out. Practice

sharing the short version, medium version, and extended version. An excellent resource to use when sharing the Gospel is the 4 Spiritual Laws, which can be downloaded from the Internet. See the link in the Sources list below.

HOW TO SAY IT

Sychar. sih-**CAR**.

Gerizim. **GAIR**-ih-zeem.

DAILY HOME BIBLE READINGS

MONDAY
Receive the Water of Life
(Revelation 21:1–7)

TUESDAY
Jesus Declares, "I Am From Above"
(John 8:21–30)

WEDNESDAY
God's Children Led by the Spirit
(Romans 8:12–17)

THURSDAY
Simon and Andrew First Disciples
(John 1:37–42)

FRIDAY
Galileans Philip and Nathanael
Become Disciples
(John 1:43–51)

SATURDAY
Jesus Heals the Son of a
Galilean Official
(John 4:43–54)

SUNDAY
Samaritans Come to Jesus
(John 4:25–42)

PREPARE FOR NEXT SUNDAY

Read **Luke 8:1-3; Mark 15:40; John 20:10-18** and next week's lesson, "Mary Magdalene: A Faithful Disciple."

Sources:

Archaeological Study Bible. Grand Rapids, Michigan: Zondervan, 2005.

Bassler, Jouette M, Harold W Attridge, Wayne A Meeks, and Society of Biblical Literature. *The HarperCollins Study Bible: Fully Revised Standard Version, with the Apocryphal/Deuterocanonical Books Student Edition*. New York: HarperCollins, 2006.

Bryant, Beauford H. and Mark S. Krause. John. *The College Press NIV Commentary*. Joplin, Missouri: College Press Publishing Company, Inc., 1998.

Gangel, Kenneth. John. *Holman New Testament Commentary*. Nashville, TN: Holman Reference, 2000.

Keener, Craig S. *The IVP Bible Background Commentary: New Testament*. Downers Grove, Illinois: InterVarsity Press, 2014.

Michaels, J. Ramsey. *The Gospel According to John. The New International Commentary on the New Testament*. Grand Rapids, Michigan: Eerdmans, 2010.

Tenney, Merrill C. John and Acts. The Expositor's Bible Commentary, Volume 9. Grand Rapids, Michigan: Zondervan, 1984.

The 4 Spiritual Laws. https://www.cru.org/us/en/how-to-know-god/would-you-like-to-know-god-personally.html

Wiersbe, Warren W. Be Alive (John 1-12). Bible Exposition Commentary. Elgin, Illinois: David C. Cook, 2009.

The Zondervan Bible Dictionary. Grand Rapids, Michigan: Zondervan, 1963. 399.

Jusu, John, Supervising Ed. *Africa Study Bible*. Calumet City: Urban Ministries, Inc.

COMMENTS / NOTES:

MARY MAGDALENE: A FAITHFUL DISCIPLE

BIBLE BASIS: Luke 8:1-3; Mark 15:40; John 20:10-18

BIBLE TRUTH: Mary Magdalene and other women were last at the Cross and first at the tomb.

MEMORY VERSE: "The twelve were with him, And certain women, which had been healed of evil spirits and infirmities, Mary called Magdalene, out of whom went seven devils" (Luke 8:1-2, KJV).

LESSON AIM: By the end of this lesson, we will DISCERN Mary Magdalene's motivations for committing her life to Jesus, APPRECIATE the sacrifices Mary Magdalene made in order to follow Jesus, and EMBRACE a lifestyle of wholehearted discipleship.

BACKGROUND SCRIPTURES: Mark 15:40; 16:1-9; Luke 8:1-3; John 20:10-18—Read and incorporate the insights gained from the Background Scriptures into your study of the lesson.

TEACHER PREPARATION

MATERIALS NEEDED: Bibles (several different versions), Quarterly Commentary/Teacher Manual, Adult Quarterly, teaching resources such as charts, worksheets/handouts, paper, pens, pencils

OTHER MATERIALS NEEDED / TEACHER'S NOTES:

_____

_____

LESSON OVERVIEW

LIFE NEED FOR TODAY'S LESSON
Being a truly committed follower of someone is often difficult, but some people reveal consistent loyalty no matter what happens. How do you show your loyalty and faithfulness? Mary Magdalene demonstrated her unwavering discipleship and loyalty to Jesus through her actions.

BIBLE LEARNING
Jesus includes women amo
followers.

BIBLE APPLICATION
Believers affirm the role
ministry.

STUDENTS' RESPONSES
Believers are loyal to Jesus, 1
cost.

LUKE 8:1-3; MARK 15:40; JOHN 20:10-18, KJV

1 And it came to pass afterward, that he went throughout every city and village, preaching and shewing the g of the kingdom of God: and ...the twelve were with him,

2 And certain women, which had been healed of evil spirits and infirmities, Mary called Magdalene, out of whom went seven devils,

3 And Joanna the wife of Chuza Herod's steward, and Susanna, and many others, which ministered unto him of their substance.

Mark 15:40 There were also women looking on afar off: among whom was Mary Magdalene, and Mary the mother of James the less and of Joses, and Salome;

John 20:10 Then the disciples went away again unto their own home.

11 But Mary stood without at the sepulchre weeping: and as she wept, she stooped down, and looked into the sepulchre,

12 And seeth two angels in white sitting, the one at the head, and the other at the feet, where the body of Jesus had lain.

13 And they say unto her, Woman, why weepest thou? She saith unto them, Because they have taken away my LORD, and I know not where they have laid him.

14 And when she had thus said, she turned herself back, and saw Jesus standing, and knew not that it was Jesus.

15 Jesus saith unto her, Woman, why weepest thou? whom seekest thou? She, supposing him to be the gardener, saith unto him, Sir, if thou have borne him hence, tell me where thou hast laid him, and I will take him away.

16 Jesus saith unto her, Mary. She turned herself, and saith unto him, Rabboni; which is to say, Master.

17 Jesus saith unto her, Touch me not; for I am not yet ascended to my Father: but go to my brethren, and say unto them, I ascend unto my Father, and your Father; and to my God, and your God.

18 Mary Magdalene came and told the disciples that she had seen the LORD, and that he had spoken these things unto her.

BIBLICAL DEFINITIONS

A. Sepulcre (**John 20:11**) *mnemion* (Gk.)—A tomb; a place of remembrance for a deceased person

B. Steward (**Luke 8:3**) *epitrophos* (Gk.)—An overseer or regent; person placed in charge of household affairs

LIGHT ON THE WORD

Demonic Possession. Demons are evil spiritual beings who are the enemies of God and His people (**Matthew 8:16; 12:43-45**). Jesus has all-power over devils and their leader, Satan. Jesus saw Satan fall from heaven like lightning (**Luke 10:18**). Demons belong to the number of fallen angels that "kept not their first estate" (**Jude 6**). Demonic possession is mentioned quite often in the New Testament; demons inflict a variety of symptoms such as deafness (**Luke 11:14**), epilepsy (**Mark 9:17**f), and insanity or behavior similar to madness (**Matthew 8:28–34**). The Gospels record that Christ distinguished between sickness and demon possession. Jesus generally healed sick people by the laying on of hands or anointing. Jesus delivered those who were demon-possessed by commanding the evil spirits to depart (for example, see **Matthew 10:8; Mark 6:13; Acts 8:7**). Sometimes people were possessed by multiple demons, such as Legion (**Mark 5:1–13**) or Mary of Magdala (**Luke 8:2**).

TEACHING THE BIBLE LESSON

LIFE NEED FOR TODAY'S LESSON

AIM: Students will correctly identify Mary Magdalene as a follower of Jesus.

INTRODUCTION

Mary Magdalene

Some traditions have erroneously advanced the idea that Mary Magdalene was a prostitute. However, recent Biblical scholars reject this label because Scripture does not support such speculation. The link between Mary and this sinful occupation may have started with the assumption that Mary Magdalene (first named in **Luke 8:2**) is the same "sinful woman" who anointed Jesus in Simon's house (**Luke 7**). But Scripture does not identify Mary Magdalene as the same woman who anointed Jesus' feet. In **Luke 8:2**, Jesus delivered Mary Magdalene from demon possession, and she became a close follower and friend of Jesus. In **Mark 15:40**, Mary was among the group of women who watched from a distance when Jesus was crucified. She was also one of the three women who brought spices to anoint Jesus' body after His burial. Mary and the women's association with Jesus, plus His appearance to the women after His Resurrection underscore one undeniable fact: Jesus valued the contributions of women in the spread of the Gospel.

BIBLE LEARNING

AIM: Students will recognize women as disciples of Jesus.

I. WOMEN WITH THE TWELVE (LUKE 8:1-3)

Luke 8:1 And it came to pass afterward, that he went throughout every city and village, preaching and shewing the glad tidings of the kingdom of God: and the twelve were with him,

With the word "afterward," Luke begins this part of his account by connecting these events to what previously ocurred. A review of **Luke 7:36-50** reveals that Jesus accepted an invitation to have dinner at the home of a Pharisee named Simon. It was here that Jesus taught a great lesson about forgiveness and demonstrated His power to forgive sins. The parallels of this account are found in **Matthew 26:6-13; Mark 14:3-9**; and **John 12:1-8** where Jesus forgave the sinful woman. He admonished Simon to have a heart of love, worship, giving, and humble submission, which were traits Jesus identified in the woman needing forgiveness.

Jesus was engaged in His Father's business of ministry to all people by proclaiming the Gospel. **Chapter 8** sheds light on the dynamic ministry of Jesus and those who traveled with Him. **Verse 1** is clear about Jesus' mission on earth: to travel extensively, preaching and showing Himself as our Redeemer, Savior, and the expected Messiah. In Greek, the phrase "shewing the glad tidings" is a single word, *euaggelo* (**ew-ang-GHEL-lo**), from which we get the English word evangelize, and is the verb form of the word usually translated "Gospel." That Jesus is the Messiah and Savior is the glad tidings. Anyone who believed in Him becomes a child of God and receives eternal life (**John 3:16**).

Jesus had many disciples (**Luke 6:13**); the ones whom He called—the twelve—traveled with Him. Luke lists these as " Simon, (whom he also named Peter,) and Andrew his brother, James and John, Philip and Bartholomew, Matthew and Thomas, James the son of Alphaeus, and Simon called Zelotes, and Judas the brother of James, and

Judas Iscariot, which also was the traitor" (**Luke 6:14-16**).

2 And certain women, which had been healed of evil spirits and infirmities, Mary called Magdalene, out of whom went seven devils, 3 And Joanna the wife of Chuza Herod's steward, and Susanna, and many others, which ministered unto him of their substance.

Verse 3 is the first reference to Joanna. She worked with Susanna and Mary Magdalene to support Jesus' ministry. Joanna was very likely present when Jesus was taken from the Cross and buried, and she is named as one of the women at the tomb on the morning of the Resurrection (**Luke 23:55; 24:10**). Joanna is a Greek form of a Hebrew name meaning "God is gracious." Joanna's discipleship was unusual because she was the wife of Chuza, Herod's "steward" (Gk. *epitrophos*, **eh-PEE-trow-foce**). This steward would be in charge of household affairs as an overseer or regent. Joanna financially supported the ministry of Jesus. Susanna's name is the Greek form of a Hebrew name meaning lily, rose, or flower. She was a woman of means, perhaps wealthy in her own right, since her husband is not mentioned. She holds a significant place in Scripture because of her dedication to Jesus.

This is the only Scripture that references Susanna by name, but certainly, she was present in other events that involved Jesus. She became one of His disciples and traveled with Him.

However, of the three women named, it is Mary Magdalene who is referred to the most in Scripture. She is portrayed as an exceptional, faithful disciple—present at the Cross, the burial, and the Resurrection as all four Gospels record (**Mathew 27:56-61; Mark 15:40, 47; 16:1-19; Luke 24:10; John 19:25, 20:1**). Mary was and continues to be

a very common name even today. During biblical times, Mary was so common that people used other descriptors for those named Mary, such as whom they were related to or where they lived. Mary was called "Magdalene" because she was from Magdala, a city in Galilee, located in the northernmost region of ancient Palestine, which is now a part of northern Israel. Magdala was a coastal area where Jesus traveled by boat after His miracle of feeding 4,000 people (**Matthew 15:39**).

Of the women in **Luke 8:1-3**, Mary Magdalene is identified first. The fact that her name is prioritized on the list of women indicates that Mary Magdalene was greatly impacted by Jesus—and she is special.

SEARCH THE SCRIPTURES

QUESTION 1
Why is the role of women in Jesus' ministry instructive for us today? In other words, what do we learn?

Answers will vary.

QUESTION 2
What is the one life experience that transformed your relationship with Jesus?

Answers will vary.

LIGHT ON THE WORD

Joanna
Joanna was a woman who had resources because of her husband's position, and she is comparable to someone today whose spouse has a high-ranking job in government, such as a secretary for a governor or district judge. Imagine Herod's reaction that his employee's wife was a disciple of Jesus This Herod is not Herod the Great who tried to kill Jesus as a small child (**Matthew 2**); he is that Herod's son, Herod Antipas, who had John the Baptist

executed (**Luke 3:19-20**). Joanna's contact with Jesus led to her deliverance and salvation. She was grateful and showed her love and devotion by supporting Jesus' ministry, despite Herod's actions against the ministry of the Gospel and the risks involved in her support.

II. WOMEN AT THE CROSS (MARK 15:40)

Each of the Gospels presents slightly different details of Jesus' death and Resurrection. The **Gospel of Mark**, which was the earliest of the four Gospels written, has the briefest account. Mark does not indicate that the disciples remained at the foot of Jesus' Cross, but he does note that there were women who looked on from a distance (**Mark 15:40**). These women included Mary Magdalene.

Mark 15:40 There were also women looking on afar off: among whom was Mary Magdalene, and Mary the mother of James the less and of Joses, and Salome;

Mark highlights the prominent roles women played in the life of Jesus as they supported His ministry. Mark identifies the women who witnessed Jesus' execution on the Cross—Mary Magdalene is mentioned again, along with Salome (**John 19:25**), and another Mary who was the mother of James "the less" and Joses. He was called "James the less" to distinguish him since James was such a common name; James the Less was younger than another James, perhaps another James in the family or among the disciples. Joses is a Greek spelling of Joseph, a common Hebrew name.

SEARCH THE SCRIPTURES

QUESTION 3
Why does the writer record the names of the women who are at the cross and at the tomb?

The writer demonstrates that women remained faithful to Jesus and were a significant part of His ministry.

QUESTION 4
How does this enhance our perspective of women in the ministry today?

Answers will vary.

LIGHT ON THE WORD
Fearless Women
Crucifixion was a humiliating and shameful death. This execution demonstrated the total power of the Roman Empire and was a lesson to Roman citizens of their fate should they offend the authorities. The women were bold to associate with Jesus. Although they were not directly at the feet of the Cross (where John records himself and Jesus' mother), the women do not hide in fear as the other disciples did. They remain, and they are the first to anoint His body on the morning of His Resurrection.

III. WOMEN AT THE TOMB (JOHN 20:10-18)

Mary Magdalene is the first to find the empty tomb, and she alerts the Apostles (**John 20:1-2**). After Peter and John return home, Mary lingers in grief. So overcome was she, that when Jesus appeared to her, she did not recognize Him. But she knew Jesus because of the distinct way He spoke to her. The miraculous had happened, and Mary was the first of Jesus' disciples to bear witness to the fact that Jesus had risen with all power in His hands. Mary could not wait to share the Good News!

John 20:10 Then the disciples went away again unto their own home. 11 But Mary stood without at the sepulchre weeping: and as she wept, she stooped down, and looked into the

108

sepulchre, **12 And seeth two angels in white sitting, the one at the head, and the other at the feet, where the body of Jesus had lain. 13 And they say unto her, Woman, why weepest thou? She saith unto them, Because they have taken away my LORD, and I know not where they have laid him.**

After seeing the empty tomb, Mary Magdalene ran to tell the disciples. Peter and John ran back with Mary to see for themselves, but soon "went away again" to their homes, perhaps to think about what they had seen. Mary Magdalene, however, stayed at the grave site, overwhelmed and distressed because she thought someone had stolen Jesus' body from the tomb. Mary didn't recognize the two angels as messengers from God, and she responded as she would to human beings. Perhaps Mary was in a state of shock and sobbing because Jesus' body should have still been there.

14 And when she had thus said, she turned herself back, and saw Jesus standing, and knew not that it was Jesus. 15 Jesus saith unto her, Woman, why weepest thou? whom seekest thou? She, supposing him to be the gardener, saith unto him, Sir, if thou have borne him hence, tell me where thou hast laid him, and I will take him away.

Mary Magdalene thought Jesus was the grounds' caretaker. When Jesus questioned her, she tearfully asked where to find Jesus' body.

16 Jesus saith unto her, Mary. She turned herself, and saith unto him, Rabboni; which is to say, Master.

Finally, when Mary Magdalene recognizes Jesus, she sees the Risen Savior! He calls her name. She answers, "Master" (Gk. *didaskalos*, **dee-DASS-kah-loce**; teacher)! The term "rabboni" is perhaps the Galilean

pronunciation of "rabbi," a Jewish title for respected religious leaders from the Hebrew "my great one." Mary acknowledges Jesus' true identity as Lord. In an instant, her mourning turns to joy.

17 Jesus saith unto her, Touch me not; for I am not yet ascended to my Father: but go to my brethren, and say unto them, I ascend unto my Father, and your Father; and to my God, and your God.

In **verse 17**, the word "touch" in Greek is *haptomai* (**HAP**-toe-my), which means to attach oneself to another. A better translation of Jesus' words to Mary would be "don't cling to me" (NLT), rather than "Touch me not" (KJV). Jesus told Mary Magdalene that He was returning to His Father, who is also her Father, and to His God, who is also her God. This is the essence of the salvation story: Jesus' sacrifice on the Cross makes Mary—and each of us—a child of God the Father.

18 Mary Magdalene came and told the disciples that she had seen the LORD, and that he had spoken these things unto her.

What a privilege for Mary Magdalene to be the one to deliver Jesus' message to the disciples—a message she received in person! Jesus delivered Mary Magdalene, and she traveled with Him in support of His ministry, witnessed His Crucifixion, and was one of the first to see Him after His resurrection. The Lord gave her unique, transformative experiences, and all believers should see her as a faithful disciple, indeed.

SEARCH THE SCRIPTURES

QUESTION 5
Why is it so beautiful that Jesus calls Mary's name?

God knows the name of each part of His creation (Isaiah 40:26). He knows the secret name of every follower who overcomes (Revelation 2:17). He knows Mary's name. He sees her. And He knows our names.

QUESTION 6

Now that we are transformed as believers, how eager are we to deliver the Gospel message to those who need Christ?

Answers will vary.

LIGHT ON THE WORD

Do You Recognize Jesus?
It should be noted that Mary was not the only one who could not recognize the resurrected Jesus. Later, Jesus shows Himself to the disciples who do not recognize Him either (**John 21:4**). Jesus' two disciples on the road to Emmaus also did not recognize Jesus until He chose to reveal His identity (**Luke 24:16, 31**). Mary Magdalene knew Jesus when He was ready for her to realize His presence.

Praise the Lord that Jesus shows Himself to those who genuinely and sincerely seek Him. He will reveal Himself in a way that often goes far beyond expectations. Mary Magdalene had a heart that honestly yearned to find Jesus, and she did. She was a devoted disciple of Jesus who demonstrated faith by her belief in Him as the Resurrected Lord.

How has the Lord revealed Himself to you? Has He spoken to you lately? Do you recognize His voice?

BIBLE APPLICATION

AIM: Students will allow their feelings to be transformed by Jesus.

Everyone who encounters Jesus after the Resurrection is transformed by His appearance. We can see a pattern in the appearances recorded by John. Mary is overcome with grief (**20:11**); the disciples are filled with fear (**v. 19**); while Thomas

doubted (**v. 25, 27**). Jesus appears right in the middle of all their feelings. God does not discount our feelings or emotions, and neither should we.

Although we are led by God's words and not led by our feelings, our feelings are important clues about the state of our hearts. Regardless of our status or condition, when we see Jesus, our hearts and feelings are transformed. Mary's sorrow turns to mission; the disciples' fear turns to joy, and Thomas' doubt turns to faith.

STUDENTS' RESPONSES

AIM: Students will share their testimonies.

Think of someone you know who has experienced a liberating transformation because of Jesus. (Maybe you have yourself.) Ask the person to share her or his testimony with you. Consider asking the person if you may record their story to share with others in your small group.

PRAYER

Heavenly Father, we are so grateful that we can call You Father because of the death and Resurrection of Jesus Christ. Thank You that Jesus paid the price for our sin so that we are reconciled—made one—with You, our Father and our God. We are committed to winning the lost . . . to seeing the demon-possessed delivered and the sick healed. Help us as we run, like Mary, with the Good News that Jesus is alive! In His Name we pray. Amen.

DIG A LITTLE DEEPER

Crises of conscience plague contemporary society. Mary Magdalene's example to us as individuals is two-fold. First, she reminds us to allow God to transform our lives. Second, she shows us what it means to be a faithful follower and friend. In a world where so much seems temporary and fleeting, Mary teaches the contemporary reader to stay plugged into our relationship with Jesus. Today's churches often find that they are bombarded with statistics of how people in younger generations are less likely to attend church. Mary's example cautions everyone not to be hasty and walk away from the empty tomb.

There's good news! Forty-seven percent of Blacks attend church once a week as compared to thrity-four percent of Whites, twenty-six percent of Asians, thirty-nine percent of Latinos, and thirty-four percent of "other" according to the Pew Research Center on Religion and Public Life. For more information, see the link in the source list.

We don't know how church attendance has been impacted since the COVID-19 Pandemic. Early statistics demonstrate that some churches have doubled or tripled in attendance, thanks to virtual or online services. There is hope!

HOW TO SAY IT

Magdala. **MAG**-dah-lah.

Salome. **SAH**-low-may.

Chuza. **KOO**-zah.

PREPARE FOR NEXT SUNDAY

Read **Acts 18:1-3, 18-21, 24-26; Romans 16:3-4** and next week's lesson, "Priscilla: Called to Minister."

DAILY HOME BIBLE READINGS

MONDAY
Jesus Appears to Paul
(1 Corinthians 15:1–11)

TUESDAY
Present with Jesus at the Cross
(John 19:25–30)

WEDNESDAY
Spices Prepared to Anoint
Jesus' Body
(Mark 16:1–8)

THURSDAY
Mary Magdalene Finds
an Empty Tomb
(John 20:1–9)

FRIDAY
Angel Confirms Jesus'
Resurrection to Women
(Matthew 28:1–10)

SATURDAY
Jesus Appears, Disciples
Sent into Ministry
(John 20:19–23)

SUNDAY
Mary Magdalene,
Faithful Disciple
(Luke 8:1-3; Mark 15:40;
John 20:10-18)

Sources:

Bassler, Jouette M, Harold W Attridge, Wayne A Meeks, and Society of Biblical Literature. The HarperCollins Study Bible: Fully Revised Standard Version, with the Apocryphal/Deuterocanonical Books Student Edition. New York: HarperCollins, 2006.

Benson, Joseph. Benson's Commentary of Old and New Testaments. Guideposts Parallel Bible, King James Version, New International Version, Living Bible and Revised Standard Version. New York: Guideposts, 1981.

Higginbotham, Evelyn Brooks. Righteous Discontent: The Women's Movement in the Black Baptist Church, 1880-1920. Cambridge, MA: Harvard University Press, 1993.

Kysar, John, R. Augsburg Commentary on the New Testament, John. Minneapolis, MN: Augsburg Fortress Publishers, 1986.

Pew Research Center: Religion & Public Life (January 30, 2009). A Religious Portrait of African-Americans. https://www.pewforum.org/2009/01/30/a-religious-portrait-of-african-americans/. Retrieved October 13, 2019.

Smith, William. Smith's Bible Dictionary. Philadelphia, PA: A.J. Holman Company, 1973.

PRISCILLA: CALLED TO MINISTER

BIBLE BASIS: Acts 18:1-3, 18-21, 24-26; Romans 16:3-4

BIBLE TRUTH: Priscilla teaches along with her husband in the early church.

MEMORY VERSE: "Greet Priscilla and Aquila my helpers in Christ Jesus: Who have for my life laid down their own necks: unto whom not only I give thanks, but also all the churches of the Gentiles" (Romans 16:3-4, KJV).

LESSON AIM: By the end of this lesson, we will RESEARCH the life and ministry of Priscilla and her husband Aquila, APPRECIATE the ministry of those who explain the way of God with accuracy, and SEEK opportunities to use our gifts or abilities to further the Gospel.

BACKGROUND SCRIPTURES: Acts 18:1-26—Read and incorporate the insights gained from the Background Scriptures into your study of the lesson.

TEACHER PREPARATION

MATERIALS NEEDED: Bibles (several different versions), Quarterly Commentary/Teacher Manual, Adult Quarterly, teaching resources such as charts, worksheets/handouts, paper, pens, pencils

OTHER MATERIALS NEEDED / TEACHER'S NOTES:

_____

_____

LESSON OVERVIEW

LIFE NEED FOR TODAY'S LESSON
Encounters that bring together people with similar gifts and talents can lead to greater opportunities for service in other arenas. How can common traits or experiences lead to a meaningful engagement in ministry or service? Priscilla and Aquila shared their tent-making business with Paul, and Paul shared his ministry of the Gospel with them.

BIBLE LEARNING
God uses women in the teaching ministry.

BIBLE APPLICATION
Christians use their God-given gifts to minister to God's people.

STUDENTS' RESPONSES
Believers affirm women's roles in the Church.

LESSON SCRIPTURE

ACTS 18:1-3, 18-21, 24-26;
ROMANS 16:3-4, KJV

1 After these things Paul departed from Athens, and came to Corinth;

2 And found a certain Jew named Aquila, born in Pontus, lately come from

Italy, with his wife Priscilla; (because that Claudius had commanded all Jews to depart from Rome:) and came unto them.

3 And because he was of the same craft, he abode with them, and wrought: for by their occupation they were tentmakers.

18 And Paul after this tarried there yet a good while, and then took his leave of the brethren, and sailed thence into Syria, and with him Priscilla and Aquila; having shorn his head in Cenchrea: for he had a vow.

19 And he came to Ephesus, and left them there: but he himself entered into the synagogue, and reasoned with the Jews.

20 When they desired him to tarry longer time with them, he consented not;

21 But bade them farewell, saying, I must by all means keep this feast that cometh in Jerusalem: but I will return again unto you, if God will. And he sailed from Ephesus.

24 And a certain Jew named Apollos, born at Alexandria, an eloquent man, and mighty in the scriptures, came to Ephesus.

25 This man was instructed in the way of the Lord; and being fervent in the spirit, he spake and taught diligently the things of the Lord, knowing only the baptism of John.

26 And he began to speak boldly in the synagogue: whom when Aquila and Priscilla had heard, they took him unto them, and expounded unto him the way of God more perfectly.

Romans 16:3 Greet Priscilla and Aquila my helpers in Christ Jesus:

4 Who have for my life laid down their own necks: unto whom not only I give thanks, but also all the churches of the Gentiles.

BIBLICAL DEFINITIONS

A. Eloquent (Acts 18:24) *logio* (Gk.)— Skilled in speech, as well as wise and learned

B. Perfectly (v. 26) *akribes* (Gk.)— Accurately, exactly, carefully

LIGHT ON THE WORD

Ephesus. A principal Roman city of Asia, Ephesus was both a strategic commercial city and a major religious center. The city was famous for its magnificent temple of Diana, one of the seven wonders of the ancient world. The practice of magic and a large part of the local economy were intertwined with this temple. Paul remained in Ephesus for three years on his third missionary journey. During this time, the Word spread throughout that region. Paul's ministry influenced fewer people to purchase magical items and images, leading to an actual riot by the merchants. After this, Paul left and went to Macedonia and returned for a brief visit with the elders several miles outside the city. Paul wrote a letter to the Ephesian church while imprisoned in Rome.

Apollos. An Alexandrian Jew who came to Ephesus in AD 52 (**Acts 18:24**). He had a profound understanding of the Old Testament but a limited understanding of Jesus. Apollos was eloquent, articulate, and enthusiastic as he preached the truth as he knew it (**Acts 18:24-25**). Priscilla and

Aquila patiently instructed Apollos, filling in the gaps in his knowledge (**Acts 18:26**). As a result, Apollos went on to become a powerful proclaimer and defender of the Christian faith (**Acts 18:27-28**).

TEACHING THE BIBLE LESSON

LIFE NEED FOR TODAY'S LESSON

AIM: Students examine Priscilla's role in the teaching ministry.

INTRODUCTION
A Tentmaker Team

Luke, the Gospel writer and author of the **Acts of the Apostles**, portrays the husband and wife team of Aquila and Priscilla as an ideal model of Christianity. They are friendly, hospitable, and generous. Aquila was a tentmaker who traveled extensively throughout the New Testament world with his wife, Priscilla (see **Acts 18:2-28; 1 Corinthians 16:19**). Some scholars suggest that Priscilla inherited wealth and held influence in her community as a possible reason she is mentioned before her husband. Most scholars support that Priscilla is mentioned before her husband because she is the primary teacher.

The Bible does not say how Paul met this couple, but it is clear that the apostle formed a friendship with Aquila and Priscilla. Through their influence and friendship, Paul was able to continue his missionary journey and left a faithful ministry team in Ephesus to preach the Gospel on his—and Jesus'—behalf.

BIBLE LEARNING

AIM: Students review the tentmakers and their ministry together.

I. PAUL MEETS PRISCILLA AND AQUILA (ACTS 18:1-3)

After Athens, Paul's next stop is Corinth, approximately fifty miles to the west. While there, Paul meets a Jewish-Christian couple named Priscilla and Aquila. Even though Aquila was born among the large Jewish population of Pontus, he and his wife had most recently lived in Italy. When Emperor Claudius commanded all Jews expelled from Rome, however, the couple left and eventually arrived in Corinth. The Scriptures affirm that Aquila, Priscilla, and Paul were tentmakers; the three worked at their trade together, which may have been how they met initially. This teaching couple also attended synagogue where Paul ministered on the Sabbath, preaching to both Jews and Gentiles.

Acts 18:1 After these things Paul departed from Athens, and came to Corinth:

Apostle Paul leaves Athens, the city whose name means "to discuss philosophy" after his debate with the philosophers and his sermon in the Areopagus (**Acts 17:16**). He arrives in Corinth at the isthmus connecting southern Greece (the Peloponnese) with northern mainland Greece along a north-south land trading route and an east-west maritime trading route. Corinth was the capital of the Roman province of Achaea. The city abounded in riches and luxury and was well-known for its debauchery. The centerpiece of the city was the temple of Aphrodite, the goddess of love and beauty, where no fewer than a thousand prostitutes provided services. Wanton sexual behavior was so prevalent in Corinth that the city's name became a verb: "to corinthianise" meant "to fornicate."

2 And found a certain Jew named Aquila, born in Pontus, lately come from Italy, with his wife Priscilla; (because that Claudius had commanded all Jews to depart from Rome:) and came unto them.

Jewish guilds kept together, whether in the street or the synagogue. Paul had little trouble finding a place to apply his trade and meet others who were similarly employed. He was in such a guild when he first met the husband-and-wife, team Priscilla and Aquila. The couple would prove to be valuable assets to the apostle's ministry.

"Aquila" is a Latin name meaning "eagle." Aquila likely took this name or was given it while he was in Rome. Aquila was born in Pontus, along the southern shore of the Black Sea. Even though this Roman province was nearly 900 miles away from Jerusalem, many Jews—including Aquila's parents—lived there. The name "Priscilla" is also Latin, and means "ancient", and therefore worthy of veneration and honor. We are not told when these Jews converted to Christianity. The couple had recently arrived in Corinth from Italy because Claudius, the Roman emperor, "had commanded all Jews to depart from Rome."

Claudius was the fourth emperor of Rome. This decree was enacted about the year AD 51 or 54 because the Jews in Rome were continually at odds with the Christians about Jesus being the Messiah. Claudius was afraid that the conflict would lead to unrest, so he banished all the Jews from Rome. At that time, Romans saw no difference between Christians and Jews, so they were all ordered to go. As a result, Priscilla and Aquila were obliged to leave Rome. When Paul found the couple, he "came unto them," visiting and staying in their home.

3 And because he was of the same craft, he abode with them, and wrought: for by their occupation they were tentmakers.

Paul shared the same skill with Aquila and Priscilla. In Greek, the phrase "same craft" is one word, *homotechnos* (hoe-**MOE**-tek-noce)—the prefix *homo*, means the same, and the suffix *technos*, means trade. Like Paul, Priscilla and Aquila were tentmakers who "wrought," or worked with their own hands to support themselves. Paul was a stranger in Corinth. He supported himself by tentmaking and would take nothing from the converts because he knew that false teachers might rise among them and accuse him of greed.

SEARCH THE SCRIPTURES
QUESTION 1
It seems coincidental that Paul, Priscilla, and Aquila are in Corinth at the same time, but their meeting is obviously God-ordained. What does this teach us about so-called "coincidence"?

Answers will vary.

QUESTION 2
How has a friendship with another Christian family or friend helped your faith journey?

Answers will vary.

LIGHT ON THE WORD
Tentmaking—Then and Now
Tentmaking was a prosperous trade. Soldier's tents consisted of a cheap yet durable cloth made from goat hair or of the leathered skins of various animals sewed together. Other tents were canopies made of linen or other materials that provided

shade in the summer to screen people from the heat of the sun. Although Paul was a scholar, he was taught a trade to earn a living like every Jewish male child.

Paul did not want anyone to accuse him of taking advantage of the people. Like Paul, Priscilla, and Aquila, many pastors today may be bi-vocational—working in a profession as they teach and minister to God's people. Such financial independence provides added income for the pastor and his family.

II. PRISCILLA AND AQUILA HELP PAUL (vv. 18-21)

Paul and his companions minister for a year and a half among the Corinthians before the stirring of the Holy Spirit prompts them to travel to Syria to further the ministry. Paul leaves, accompanied by Priscilla and Aquila, and sails back across the Aegean Sea.

The ship upon which the trio is traveling stops in Ephesus for a short time and Paul takes advantage of the stopover to teach in the local Jewish synagogue. His preaching stirs interest among the Jewish inhabitants of Ephesus, who entreat Paul to stay with them longer. However, Paul desires to return to Jerusalem in time for one of the Jewish festivals and is unable to stay. He promises, however, to return if God will permit it. He also leaves Priscilla and Aquila in Ephesus to carry on what he has begun. Priscilla and Aquila remain in Ephesus for several years and permit their home to be used as the meeting place for the Christian church they help to plant.

18 And Paul after this tarried there yet a good while, and then took his leave of the brethren, and sailed thence into Syria, and with him Priscilla and Aquila; having shorn his head in Cenchrea: for he had a vow.

While teaching a good number of those gathering in the synagogue weekly, Paul "tarried" (Gk. *prosmeno*, pros-**MEH**-no) meaning "to continue" or "to remain with" them for an unspecified length of time, which is understood to be several days. Paul stayed, preaching and teaching among them, even after a plot to kill him had failed (**18:12-17**). Because the people were receptive, the preached Word was effectual in convicting and convincing that Jesus is the Christ. Note that in the previous verse, those gathered were called Jews and Greeks. After Paul's effective and persuasive ministry to them, he now calls them "brethren" (Gk. *adelphotes*, ah-del-**FOE**-tace), which explicitly means a brother by birth, national origin, or friendship. However, within the Christian community, the term became all-inclusive to refer to those who believed, whether Jew or Greek, bond or free, and male or female.

The "vow" (Gk. *euche*, yew-**KHAY**) that Paul made earlier was probably a 30-day fast and prayer of thanksgiving to God when he did not shave. Shaving his head was simply an outward Jewish expression of his inward sincerity when this period of consecration had ended. Cenchrae was the port city nearest to Corinth, where they actually embarked to sail across the Aegean Sea.

19 And he came to Ephesus, and left them there: but he himself entered into the synagogue, and reasoned with the Jews.

The Roman city Ephesus was located on the sea between Smyrna and Miletus (the place from which Paul would call the elders of the church). While in port at Ephesus,

Paul left his companions, Priscilla and Aquila, and went directly to the synagogue to again debate with the Jewish religious and philosophical leaders assembled there. Paul was ever ready and ever seeking to persuade, convince, debate, and prove that Jesus Christ is the Messiah.

The Greek word *sunagoge* (soo-nah-go-GAY) is used in various grammatical forms. As a verb, "to synagogue" means "to bring together" as in a harvest or a group of men. As a noun, "synagogue" is a formal assembly of Jewish men who met every Sabbath and feast day to pray, read, and discuss Scripture. Christians also adapted the word "synagogue" to describe their formal gathering in the early church. "Synagogue" also refers to the very buildings where these religious Jewish assemblies, as well as trials, were held. There was usually one synagogue in every town that had at least ten Jewish men.

20 When they desired him to tarry longer time with them, he consented not; 21 But bade them farewell, saying, I must by all means keep this feast that cometh in Jerusalem: but I will return again unto you, if God will. And he sailed from Ephesus.

Paul's teaching was so effective that Jewish religious leaders, some of whom were new converts to Christianity, asked him to stay or "tarry" (a related, but slightly different Greek verb than "tarry" in **v. 18**) with them a while longer. Paul declined their request that he extend his stay.

Paul explained that he must go to Jerusalem, the place of worship. The Jews had three "pilgrimage feasts" (Passover, Tabernacles, and Pentecost) which, if at all possible, were supposed to be celebrated at the Temple in Jerusalem. As a dedicated ethnic Jew, Paul wished to attend. He had set out with

this goal and held fast to his conviction to move on; however, he did leave them with a caveat. He promised to return only if God were willing. "God willing," was a shared understanding among the pious Jews and Greeks.

SEARCH THE SCRIPTURES

QUESTION 3
Why is teamwork and partnership vital to ministry success?

Answers will vary.

QUESTION 4
Compare and contrast teaching and preaching.

Answers will vary.

LIGHT ON THE WORD
Partnership in Ministry
Teamwork and partnership in ministry are empowering, encouraging, and refining. The Bible says that iron sharpens iron (**Proverbs 27:17**), and working in tandem with others perfects our efforts. Sermons and lessons are better when teams work together to coordinate the message, music, and digital aspects.

As believers, we should seek accountability and value one another—both male and female. In this account, like other lessons this quarter, women are mentioned as central in the spread of the Gospel, and women continue to be central to the work of the ministry today.

III. PRISCILLA AND AQUILA TEACH APOLLOS (VV. 24-26)

Sometime later, Apollos, a Jew who was born in Alexandria, comes to Ephesus. Apollos, described as "an eloquent man, and mighty in the Scriptures" (**v. 24**), was excited about the Word of God and the Lord Jesus Christ.

Apollos possessed excellent teaching skills. He taught the Word diligently, even though he only knew about the baptism of John. Apollos' ministry caught the attention of Priscilla and Aquila. They were impressed with his teaching and his boldness in the synagogue, but they realize that Apollos lacked a fuller understanding of Jesus.

24 And a certain Jew named Apollos, born at Alexandria, an eloquent man, and mighty in the scriptures, came to Ephesus.

After Paul's departure from Ephesus, while Priscilla and Aquila were there, one of John the Baptist's disciples named Apollos arrived in the city and began preaching the Word. Apollos was a cultured, educated Jew from Alexandria, a thriving Egyptian metropolis that was home to a significant number of Jews who were lead scholars of their day. "Apollos" is a Greek name that honors the youthful god of music and light.

Luke describes the young man as being "eloquent." The Greek word for eloquence is *logios* (**LOW**-gee-oce), which means skilled in speech as well as wise and learned. Apollos was also "mighty" in Scriptures. In this case, the Greek adjective *dunatos* (doo-nah-**TOCE**) means capable or excellent, rather than strong or powerful. The word "Scriptures" refers to the Old Testament, the only written revelation from God about Himself at that time. Apollos had thoroughly read, carefully examined, could readily cite, had vast knowledge of, and was capable of explaining the Scriptures.

25 This man was instructed in the way of the Lord; and being fervent in the spirit, he spake and taught diligently

the things of the Lord, knowing only the baptism of John.

The word "instructed" suggests that Apollos' parents, who may have been disciples of John, trained Apollos in the Scriptures. But Apollos had only been taught the rudiments of the Christian faith, here called the "way of the Lord." Apollos knew of Christ, but he did not know Christ as Lord and Savior. Despite his incomplete training, Apollos was "fervent" (Gk. *zeo*, **ZEH**-oh), boiling with enthusiasm to preach the Good News. The word "spirit" in this case refers to Apollos' own spirit; in other words, his soul burned with zeal for the glory of God, and he "diligently" (Gk. *akribos*, ah-kree-**BOCE**) proclaimed the Word according to the measure of grace and knowledge he had received.

The phrase "knowing only the baptism of John" must be understood as the entire ministry of John, including John's doctrine of repentance and remission of sins, which looked forward to the Christ who was to come as well as to His baptism. Scholars are not in agreement, but whatever Apollos was lacking he received from Priscilla and Aquila.

26 And he began to speak boldly in the synagogue: whom when Aquila and Priscilla had heard, they took him unto them, and expounded unto him the way of God more perfectly.

Apollos spoke out boldly in the synagogue without fear of the Jews. While attending a synagogue meeting, Priscilla and Aquila hear Apollo preach and observe some deficiency in his message. With godly concern for the young minister's message, they take him aside and privately teach him, explaining the Word to him more thoroughly. The word "more perfectly" is from the Greek word *akribes* (ah-kree-BASE) and means more accurately. It is related to "diligently" in the previous verse. When Apollos preached an incomplete way of the Lord diligently, Priscilla and Aquila taught him more diligently. In other words, Priscilla and Aquila supplied the knowledge that Apollos was lacking. Later, Apollos would become one of Paul's trusted friends and companions (**1 Corinthians 16:12; Titus 3:13**).

SEARCH THE SCRIPTURES

QUESTION 5
Why are Priscilla and Aquila courageous?

It takes courage to correct someone.

QUESTION 6
Why is Apollos rewarded for his humility?

Apollos became a better teacher because he was willing to be corrected by Priscilla and Aquila.

LIGHT ON THE WORD
Training Teachers
Priscilla and Aquila taught the eloquent speaker, Apollos. What Apollos learned made his ministry even more powerful. We all need teachers or mentors who can help us expound the Word of God effectively. Accepting correction from those who may be more spiritually mature takes humility. In the end, we gain a better understanding of how to teach the Scriptures, which causes God's Word to prosper, winning more souls to the Kingdom.

IV. PAUL SALUTES PRISCILLA AND AQUILA (ROMANS 16:3-4)
At the close of his letter to the Romans, the Apostle Paul greets 26 people by name.

At the top of this list is the ministry team, Priscilla and Aquila. He refers to the couple as "my helpers in Christ Jesus." The word "helper" means "fellow worker" and looks back to their love and aid when Paul arrived in Corinth. The apostle says that the couple "laid down their own necks," or risked their lives on his behalf. Scripture does not record the incident when this took place, but at some point the couple was willing to sacrifice their own lives for the Gospel. Paul affirms his gratitude for this couple's work, adding that "also all the churches of the Gentiles" thank them. This shows that Paul considers Priscilla and Aquila's work so influential that every church started by non-Jews owes gratitude to them.

Romans 16:3 Greet Priscilla and Aquila my helpers in Christ Jesus: 4 Who have for my life laid down their own necks: unto whom not only I give thanks, but also all the churches of the Gentiles.

Aquila was born in Pontus, moved to Rome at some point, was exiled from Rome around AD 52, lived in Corinth, journeyed from Corinth to Ephesus with Paul, stayed there long enough to help establish a church, and then apparently moved back to Rome and hosted a house church there too.

The date that the couple left Ephesus and returned to Rome is unknown, but at that time either Claudius had died or his edict that ordered the Jews to depart from Rome had been revoked. The couple returned to Rome, and they were there when the apostle wrote this epistle to the church in Rome. Paul salutes them and refers to them as "my helpers in Christ Jesus." The term "helpers" translates the Greek *sunergos* (soon-air-GOCE), which could also be translated "co-workers" or "fellow laborers." They are not just lesser helpers in Paul's great ministry; they toil equally alongside the apostle. The couple assisted Paul in spreading the Gospel and promoting the kingdom and Lordship of Christ. They helped encourage young converts and comfort them with their own experiences and therefore they were greatly appreciated by the apostle in the work of the Lord Jesus.

When Paul says that Priscilla and Aquila have "for my life laid down their necks," he is intimating that the couple exposed themselves to great danger to save his life. The allusion is to the ancient practice of beheading and someone laying down his head and offering his neck to the executioner in place of another. Today, we might say someone "stuck their neck out for me." We should not suppose that Priscilla and Aquila literally did this, but the expression intends that in some way they risked their own lives for Paul's.

We are given no further details of this courageous act, but there are a couple of plausible possibilities. The incident may have occurred at the insurrection in Corinth when the Jews dragged Paul to the judgment seat of Galileo and beat Sosthenes, the ruler of the synagogue before him (**Acts 18:17**). Otherwise, it might have been in Ephesus, where Demetrius and the craftsmen incited a riot against Paul and his companions (**Acts 19:24**). Aquila and Priscilla were present at both events and were no doubt actively protecting the apostle. Whatever the case, Paul was very grateful for their heroic assistance.

With his missionary work all over the Mediterranean, Paul knows that the church is growing and flourishing not just because of his own teaching, but also through the work of other faithful Christ-followers. Paul shares his gratitude for this couple who have sheltered him and continue to shelter the church (both in Ephesus and in Rome). He sends not only his thanks but also the thanks of all "Gentile" churches. The word "Gentile" here is *ethnos* (Gk. ETH-noce), which is often correctly translated as Gentile as opposed to Jewish. However, the word can also denote people groups everywhere. What a tribute that Priscilla and Aquila received gratitude from all over the Christian world for their diligent work for the Lord!

SEARCH THE SCRIPTURES

QUESTION 5
Who are the people in your life you would consider to be co-laborers? In what way do you work together to spread the message of the Gospel?

Answers will vary.

QUESTION 6
For which people or causes would you be willing to "stick out your neck"? What makes these people or causes worth the risk?

Answers will vary.

BIBLE APPLICATION

AIM: Students value Christian marriage as a partnership in ministry.

Christian homes and solid Christian marriages remain two of the best tools for spreading the Gospel. Husband-and-wife teams can be tremendous blessings for the body of Christ. The faithfulness of people like Priscilla and Aquila makes ministry a joy for others.

The effectiveness of their ministry is a tribute to their personal relationship with each other and with God. Their hospitality became the doorway of salvation for many, which is why the enemy fights so hard against marriage.

More than half the marriages in the United States—and in the church—end in divorce. List some of the positive features and negative hindrances that can affect husband-and-wife businesses/partnerships (and marriages). Report on your list next week.

STUDENTS' RESPONSES

AIM: Students will commit to mentoring, or to being mentored.

In today's lesson, Priscilla and Aquila took young Apollos under their wing and mentored him in the Gospel. Examine your life to see whom you might influence in the body of Christ. If you can't think of anyone, ask God to help you encourage someone this week. Call or write and lift that person's spirit.

PRAYER

We thank You, Father, for the example of Priscilla and Aquila who worked in the ministry together. Strengthen the marriages of those who labor in the vineyard on Your behalf. Thank You for our pastor and his wife and those who lead and teach. Give them wisdom, willing hands to help, and listening ears to hear one another's hearts. In the Name of Jesus, we pray. Amen.

DIG A LITTLE DEEPER

Bishop Glenn and Dr. Pauline Plummer are Christian teachers with a world-wide impact! As Bishop and First Lady to Israel for the Church Of God In Christ, here is an excellent example of partnership in ministry.

Since 1999, Bishop Plummer has served as the Senior Pastor at Ambassadors for Christ Church in Detroit, Michigan. Together, he and his wife model team-teaching in their weekly YouTube program, The Lesson Official, where they expound on the upcoming Sunday school lesson based on the International Lesson Series.

The Plummers' expansive ministry also includes a national broadcast, which can be accessed on YouTube. Their's is a preaching/teaching model for couples that, "Two are better than one, because they have a good return for their labor," (**Ecclesiastes 4:9, JKV**).

To connect with this dynamic duo, email: cogicisrael@gmail.com or thelessonofficial@gmail.com. May God continue to bless their marriage as they minister...*together!*

HOW TO SAY IT

Cenchrae. kenn-**KRAY**-ah.

Sosthenes. **SOSS**-theh-neez.

Aquila. ah-**QUILL**-ah.

DAILY HOME BIBLE READINGS

MONDAY
Paul Reflects on His Ministry
(2 Timothy 4:9–18)

TUESDAY
Greetings to Saints in Jesus Christ
(Colossians 4:7–15)

WEDNESDAY
The Holy Kiss Strengthens
Ministry Bond
(2 Corinthians 13:11–13;
1 Thessalonians 5:23–28)

THURSDAY
Ministry Shifts from Jews to Gentiles
(Acts 18:4–11)

FRIDAY
Roman Official Refuses to Settle
Dispute
(Acts 18:12–17)

SATURDAY
Greetings to All Sisters in Ministry
(Romans 16:1–2, 6–7, 12–13, 16)

SUNDAY
Priscilla, Key Outreach Minister
(Acts 18:1–3, 18–21, 24–26;
Romans 16:3–4)

PREPARE FOR NEXT SUNDAY

Read **Acts 16:11-15,40; 1 Corinthians
1:26-30** and next week's lesson, "Lydia:
Called to Serve."

Sources:
Achtemeier, Paul. *Harper's Bible Dictionary*. New York: HarperCollins,
1985. 173, 182-3.
Strong, James. *The New Strong's Exhaustive Concordance of the Bible*.
Nashville, TN: Thomas Nelson, 2003.
Thayer, Joseph Henry. *A Greek-English Lexicon of the New Testament*.
New York: American Book Company, 1994.
Vine, W.E. *Vine's Complete Expository Dictionary of Old and New
Testament Words*. Nashville, TN: Thomas Nelson, 1996.

COMMENTS / NOTES:

LYDIA: CALLED TO SERVE

BIBLE BASIS: Acts 16:11-15, 40; 1 Corinthians 1:26-30

BIBLE TRUTH: Lydia responds to the Gospel and becomes and example of hospitality.

MEMORY VERSE: "And when she was baptized, and her household, she besought us, saying, If ye have judged me to be faithful to the Lord, come into my house, and abide there. And she constrained us" (Acts 16:15, KJV).

LESSON AIM: By the end of this lesson, we will ASSESS how Lydia used her gifts and her place in society to support Paul's ministry, REPENT of the times we have looked down on others who have not had the same opportunities or advantages, and SERVE others joyfully through whatever means are at our disposal.

BACKGROUND SCRIPTURES: ACTS 16:11-15, 40—Read and incorporate the insights gained from the Background Scriptures into your study of the lesson.

TEACHER PREPARATION

MATERIALS NEEDED: Bibles (several different versions), Quarterly Commentary/Teacher Manual, Adult Quarterly, teaching resources such as charts, worksheets/handouts, paper, pens, pencils

OTHER MATERIALS NEEDED / TEACHER'S NOTES:

_____

_____

LESSON OVERVIEW

LIFE NEED FOR TODAY'S LESSON
Many people have been recipients of generous hospitality or have been in a position to extend hospitality to someone. In what ways can openness and a listening ear provide opportunities to serve? Lydia was an attentive woman who responded to the Gospel message with faithfulness and generous hospitality.

BIBLE LEARNING
God chooses women to provide a gathering place for the Apostle Paul and his ministry team.

BIBLE APPLICATION
Believers model Lydia's welcoming spirit.

STUDENTS' RESPONSES
Believers are hospitable.

LESSON SCRIPTURE

ACTS 16:11-15, 40;
1 CORINTHIANS 1:26-30, KJV

11 Therefore loosing from Troas, we came with a straight course to Samothracia, and the next day Neapolis;

12 And from thence to Philippi, which is the chief city of that part of Macedonia, and a colony: and we were in that city abiding certain days.

13 And on the sabbath we went out of the city by a river side, where prayer was wont to be made; and we sat down, and spake unto the women which resorted thither.

14 And a certain woman named Lydia, a seller of purple, of the city of Thyatira, which worshipped God, heard us: whose heart the Lord opened, that she attended unto the things which were spoken of Paul.

15 And when she was baptized, and her household, she besought us, saying, If ye have judged me to be faithful to the Lord, come into my house, and abide there. And she constrained us.

40 And they went out of the prison, and entered into the house of Lydia: and when they had seen the brethren, they comforted them, and departed.

1 Corinthians 1:26 For ye see your calling, brethren, how that not many wise men after the flesh, not many mighty, not many noble, are called:

27 But God hath chosen the foolish things of the world to confound the wise; and God hath chosen the weak things of the world to confound the things which are mighty;

28 And base things of the world, and things which are despised, hath God chosen, yea, and things which are not, to bring to nought things that are:

29 That no flesh should glory in his presence.

30 But of him are ye in Christ Jesus, who of God is made unto us wisdom, and righteousness, and sanctification, and redemption:

BIBLICAL DEFINITIONS

A. Prayer (Acts 16:13) *proseuche* (Gk.)—A call to God, or a place to call on God

B. Faithful (v. 15) *pistos* (Gk.)—Trustworthy and reliable

LIGHT ON THE WORD

Purple Cloth. The ancient Mediterranean peoples used a dye from a certain kind of sea snail found in the eastern Mediterranean Sea. This dye was costly because of its rarity and the labor intensity of extracting the dye. Clothing made from this dye was equally expensive and reserved for notable members of society. The color is now called Tyrean purple, after Tyre, the Phoenician city that perhaps discovered the dye.

Philippi. A predominantly Roman city at this time, Philippi was eight miles inland from Neapolis, which was a seaport in northern Macedonia. The city is named for Alexander the Great's father, Philip II of Macedon. The city, Philippi, was located near two rivers and connected with coastal cities by several roads that facilitated trade. The area was financially lucrative. Philippi lay along the Egnatian Way, the major east-west Roman road connecting lands in Greece and Turkey.

TEACHING THE BIBLE LESSON

LIFE NEED FOR TODAY'S LESSON

AIM: Students consider the twists and turns of ministry and church planting.

INTRODUCTION
Church Planting
Paul and Barnabas successfully planted many churches in Syria and the surrounding provinces. Now, they were on a new journey

to plant churches throughout the Roman province of Asia. Paul and Silas set out from Antioch and were joined by Timothy while visiting a previously established church in Lystra. Soon after, the Holy Spirit altered the group's plans to go into Asia and guided the men instead to Macedonia. At this point, Luke (the writer of **Acts**) joined the team, and they set sail from the eastern shore of the Aegean Sea.

In Philippi, where they are preaching, the team meets Lydia. They cast a demon out of a slave girl, and her masters provoke an uproar that ends with the arrest of Paul and Silas. In jail, the prisoners sing, and God sends an earthquake to shake open the doors of every cell. The chains also fall off, freeing Paul and Silas. Fearful that he is going to be punished for the escape of his inmates, the jailer is about to kill himself until Paul and Silas assure him that all prisoners are still there. The two apostles teach the jailer about Jesus Christ, and he—and his household—are saved.

Throughout their ministry, Paul and Silas benefited from the hospitality of wealthy converts, but Paul also knew that most Christians supported him with sacrificial giving. Paul wrote to the Corinthian church to encourage them.

BIBLE LEARNING

AIM: Students welcome worshippers who are different.

I. THE COLONY AT PHILIPPI (ACTS 16:11-13)

It took two to five days for Paul and his team to travel from Troas to Macedonia. The first colony they visited in Macedonia was Philippi. On the Sabbath, Paul and the

others with him made their way through the city gate to the water's edge. They had discovered that there was no synagogue in Philippi, probably because the community did not have ten Jewish men living there, which was the requirement for a synagogue. Down by the riverside, women gathered to worship, draw water, do laundry, and enjoy female companionship.

Paul and his friends began to preach Christ to these women. Paul had learned that God did not show favoritism, and the women who had converted to Christ both supported and spread the Gospel in concert with Paul's ministry.

11 Therefore loosing from Troas, we came with a straight course to Samothracia, and the next day to Neapolis; 12 And from thence to Philippi, which is the chief city of that part of Macedonia, and a colony: and we were in that city abiding certain days.

As the disciples set sail from Troas, even the wind was in their favor. With smooth sailing, their's was a straight course that took two days. They traveled to the island of Samothracia and stayed overnight. The next day, they sailed to Neapolis. There, they journeyed on foot to their destination—the great city of Philippi.

Paul and his companions lodged in the city for several days. No one contacted them. In the past, when the apostles entered new territory, someone was there to meet and greet them (**Acts 11:26; 13:14-15**). However, the Jewish community had not yet spread from Jerusalem to Macedonia.

13 And on the sabbath we went out of the city by a river side, where

prayer was wont to be made; and we sat down, and spake unto the women which resorted thither.

The Sabbath is Saturday, the seventh day of the week, which was a sacred day when the Israelites were required to abstain from all work. On the Sabbath, it was customary for Paul and all Jews to gather for worship, prayer, and read the Scriptures in the synagogue. There was no synagogue of the Jews in Philippi, but the women were still determined to worship God.

They met outside the city at a river, which was probably the Gangites River, a mile or two west of Philippi. The apostle found a small group of proselytized women praying, and joined them for worship. The Greek noun *proseuche* (pros-yew-**KHAY**) or "prayer," describes both a prayer addressed to God and a place of prayer. Traditionally, Jews were supposed to wash their hands before prayer, and the river would certainly provide water for such cleansing. The disciples shared the Good News about Jesus Christ with women.

Lydia and the gathering of women became the first European converts to our Christian faith. May women's work and women's worship ever be heralded in the annals of biblical and local church history as integral, not incidental, to the Good News—to the Gospel preached, taught, and believed!

SEARCH THE SCRIPTURES

QUESTION 1
God directed Paul and his team to join the women's worship service at the river. Why is this significant?

Women are integral—not incidental—to the Church.

QUESTION 2
Why was the river a perfect place to worship in the absence of a synagogue?

The women were able to follow the ritual of washing before prayer.

LIGHT ON THE WORD
Macedonia
This region of Macedonia is a Roman colony and populated mostly by Roman citizens. Far from the center of Rome, this region was a military conquest that was a part of the Roman Empire.

The inhabitants of such colonies were protected and governed by Roman laws. Paul and Silas will use their status as Roman citizens to embarrass the leaders of the city when they are thrown into prison.

II. THE CONVERSION OF LYDIA (vv. 14-15, 40)

When Paul begins to speak, Lydia listens and accepts the truth, and she becomes the first convert in Europe. She is baptized along with her entire household into the Christian community of believers. The joy she experienced in Christ must have been tremendous because she invites Paul and his companions to stay in her home as her guests and refused to let them say no.

Paul and the other missionaries traveling with him stayed with Lydia until their ministry in the city had concluded. Her home became the first church at Philippi. Paul later referred to the Philippian church as his "joy and crown" (**Philippians 4:1**).

Lydia became one of Paul's financial supporters and was a loyal helper in his ministry. Lydia even fearlessly opened her house church to Paul and Silas after they were released from prison. She did not let the fear of associating with people accused of rabble-rousing keep her from supporting God's workers.

14 And a certain woman named Lydia, a seller of purple, of the city of Thyatira, which worshipped God, heard us: whose heart the Lord opened, that she attended unto the things which were spoken of Paul.

Lydia was a woman of Thyatira, the city of commerce in western Asia Minor. It was well-known throughout the region for its dyer's guild and textiles. Thyatira is a far distance from Philippi—nearly 400 miles. We are never told why she is living in Philippi.

Roman law did not prevent women, whether freeborn or former slaves, from engaging in business enterprises on their own. No husband was mentioned along with Lydia, so she was likely a widow since a woman who had not yet married would not live on her own. To support herself without a husband, Lydia was a "seller of purple," either the dye or cloth dyed this color. Such cloth was an expensive luxury, used for official Roman garments. Hers was a noble profession.

The name Lydia is Greek, and Thyatira is in a region of Asia Minor that had been thoroughly Hellenized. It is therefore likely that Lydia was a Gentile. She does, however, worship (Gk. *sebo*, **SEH**-bo) the One True God, a word often used to connote a Jewish proselyte (**Acts 13:43, 17:4, 18:7**). Lydia worshiped God with the knowledge she had. When she heard the truth of the Gospel, the Lord opened her heart, and she wanted to know more about Jesus. While attending this prayer gathering, Lydia welcomed the opportunity to hear the apostles teach. As she learned about the God she worshiped, she accepted into her heart Jesus Christ, God's Son.

15 And when she was baptized, and her household, she besought us, saying, If ye have judged me to be faithful to the Lord, come into my house, and abide there. And she constrained us.

Lydia's response to the Gospel of Christ Jesus was to be baptized. Lydia's baptism and that of her household marked the beginning of the Philippian church. "Baptized" (Gk. *baptizo*, bap-**TEED**-zo) means to submerge in water. Since they were already gathered at the riverside, it was convenient to baptize Lydia and her household following their conversion. Lydia's entire household— made up of family members and servants— heard the Good News, believed, and were baptized. Baptism into the Christian family is a cause for celebration!

After becoming a baptized member of the family of God, Lydia extended hospitality to her new found family—the apostles. She was very grateful to Paul, Silas, and Luke, and wanted to show her gratitude by inviting them to stay in her home with her and her family. Although her quantifiable wealth is not recorded, evidently Lydia had the means to accommodate Paul and his companions comfortably.

The apostles were reluctant because they did not want to impose. However, Lydia insisted that they stay. She was so emphatic that she "constrained" (Gk. *parabiazomai*, pah-rah-bee-**ODD**-zo-my), or made a persuasive appeal for them to stay at her home while in Philippi. Central to this plea was Lydia's assertion that the apostles found her "faithful" (Gk. *pistos*, peese-**TOCE**), meaning trustworthy and reliable.

Lydia extended a hospitality paradigm that is simple to follow: Show kindness to one another, especially to those in the household of faith (**Galatians 6:10**). When the disciples accepted Lydia's hospitality, she and her family and servants, as well as her Philippian neighbors, had the opportunity to receive more teaching of the Good News, share in discipleship, and help birth a new Christian community.

40 And they went out of the prison, and entered into the house of Lydia: and when they had seen the brethren, they comforted them, and departed.

After establishing an enthusiastic following in Philippi and leading many to Christ, Paul and Silas are arrested. They cast a demon out of a girl, but this interfered with her master's income. The master complained to the leaders of the city that Paul's group was preaching an illegal message under Roman law. Romans disapproved of any religion that did not make allowances for the divinity of the emperor; Paul and Silas were beaten and imprisoned.

While in chains, Paul and Silas sing praises to the Lord, and at midnight, an earthquake rocks them free. The jailer and his entire family become Christians. After their release, Paul raises objections to his treatment, which should not have been allowed since Paul was a Roman citizen. Although he had not caused a political or legal stir before imprisonment, he did so afterward.

Our passage continues once Paul and Silas leave prison. They head to Lydia's house church and experience the same hospitality they did at her conversion. Lydia knows their character and knows they did nothing to deserve a beating or jail time. The missionary team recognizes the rest of the town is too hostile to them and decides to leave, but they know Lydia will provide them with one last stay of hospitality. Lydia is not afraid of her reputation for associating with these men. She takes her stand with God's men, regardless of the consequences.

SEARCH THE SCRIPTURES

QUESTION 3
Why is Lydia's conversion so significant to the ministry of Paul, Silas, and Luke?

Lydia's home was the location of the church at Philippi.

QUESTION 4

What effort have you made to lead your family and close friends to Christ?

Answers will vary.

LIGHT ON THE WORD
A Heart For God
It is not enough to worship God the Father. We must believe in Jesus Christ, His Son. There is no acceptance by God except through Jesus Christ as Mediator. God offers us salvation by His grace through faith in Jesus Christ.

Jesus stands at the door to our hearts. It is up to each individual to open his or her heart to the Lord. The choice is ours. God touched Lydia's heart. She believed the Gospel of Jesus Christ, and she was saved.

Lydia's enthusiastic and attentive listening was fertile ground for God to open her heart to understand and accept the Gospel. The "heart" (Gk. *kardia*, kar-**DEE**-ah) represents the soul or mind as the resident place of one's thoughts, passions, desires, appetites, affections, purposes, understanding, intelligence, will, character, and intentions. Lydia's "open heart surgery" was appreciably more than an emotional response to a well-crafted sermon and loquacious rhetoric. As she listened, Lydia engaged her thoughts, affections, and understanding about God to believe in Christ Jesus! While Lydia had been seeking God, God was seeking her—and this nation.

III. THE CROSS' POWER (1 CORINTHIANS 1:26-28)

God does not hesitate to call women to spread the Word. Lydia was rich, but many converts were poor or working class. Paul tells these converts that formal education, political power, and economic status are not the requirements in the kingdom of God.

1 Corinthians 1:26 For ye see your calling, brethren, how that not many wise men after the flesh, not many mighty, not many noble, are called:

These verses from **1 Corinthians**, one of several letters Paul wrote to the church at Corinth, explain how to live in unity and holiness before God. God calls us to offer what we have to one another. Lydia had a place where the missionary team could stay, so she offers it.

The Corinthian believers thought they had wisdom, strength, and social standing to offer God. Paul reminds them that while such things are impressive and perhaps even helpful to the world's viewpoint, to God, they are weak. Paul outright tells the Corinthian church that they do not have the socially admired attributes they think they have. They are not wise or strong or powerful. And yet God calls them.

27 But God hath chosen the foolish things of the world to confound the wise; and God hath chosen the weak things of the world to confound the things which are mighty; 28 And base things of the world, and things which are despised, hath God chosen, yea, and things which are not, to bring to nought things that are:

Even though Paul writes that the Corinthian church has nothing much to offer God, he also asserts that God specifically chooses those without much to offer to do His work. The foolish confound the wise. God makes Jesus our wisdom (**v. 30**), and we are in Christ, so we do not need to worry about how much wisdom we have. We will have the knowledge we need when we are unified with Christ.

The weak confound the mighty by the work of God. The "base" things are the elementary things—things so obvious and common that no one regards them. These "base" things are what God chooses. "Things which are not" means "things that do not exist" and is paired with the phrase "things that are," meaning "things that do exist."

God uses those who are considered by some as lowly and despised. The "things which are not" may refer to things that don't exist, but God brings "to nought" or nothing the things people considered necessary.

This is a reference to systems of behavior and interaction that are powerless in light of God's power. God gives us the strength we need to make a difference in our world.

SEARCH THE SCRIPTURES

QUESTION 5
Why is Paul's message to Corinth a wise summary of this lesson?

Answers will vary.

QUESTION 6
How has God used the weaknesses in your life to show His glory?

Answers will vary.

LIGHT ON THE WORD
What About You?
God chooses explicitly those whom the world disregards to show His glory. The Lord ordained twelve social outcasts to be His disciples and learn from Him. Empowered with the Holy Spirit, they, in turn, were responsible for sharing the message of the Cross worldwide.

Perceived as a powerless baby born in a manger, Jesus escaped the murderous rampage of a king. A despised Cross and physical death, instead of ending Jesus' existence, demonstrated His wisdom and power over sin and the grave itself. You, too, have the power of the Holy Spirit living inside of you. Why not allow God to use you?

BIBLE APPLICATION
AIM: Students practice hospitality.

Missionaries and those who travel to Africa report on the beauty of hospitality throughout much of the continent. Whenever anyone needs food or shelter, the members of the church take them into their own homes until they can correct whatever problem might have caused their circumstance. Such hospitality is not uncommon across the world. Many Christians in America practice hospitality, too. What are some examples that you have seen in your church or community?

STUDENTS' RESPONSES
AIM: Students will use their gifts to continue the ministry of Jesus Christ.

Through Lydia's successful trade of purple, God provided for her to house Paul's team. How has God equipped you? Find a way to use your gifts to continue the work of ministry this week, and just like Lydia, don't take "No" for an answer!

PRAYER
Father, we are inspired by Lydia's example to use all that we have for heaven's sake. Thank You for giving us talents and resources to continue spreading the Good News of Jesus Christ. May we remain attentive to your voice and obedient to do whatever the Holy Spirit guides us to do this week. In the Name of Jesus, we pray. Amen.

DIG A LITTLE DEEPER
The early church started in homes, often called house churches. These small groups are where teaching and spiritual growth occurred. Today, we call this process "discipleship."

Many Sunday school classes function as discipleship groups and, like Lydia's home, are the perfect setting for Bible study. Attendees usually feel more comfortable studying together and asking questions here than in larger groups. Intimate settings promote accountability and are ideal for individuals to mature spiritually. Search the Internet for small group guidelines.

HOW TO SAY IT

Troas. **TROE**-as.

Samothrace. **SAH**-moe-thray-ss.

Neapolis. nee-**AH**-poe-liss.

Thyatira. thigh-ah-**TIE**-rah.

DAILY HOME BIBLE READINGS

MONDAY
Don't Complain but Serve
One Another
(1 Peter 4:7–11)

TUESDAY
Everyday Expressions of Hospitality
(Romans 12:9–19)

WEDNESDAY
Hospitality Practiced in Jail
and Home
(Acts 16:35–40)

THURSDAY
Hospitality Practiced by Widow
and Bishop
(1 Timothy 5:9–10, 3:2)

FRIDAY
Christ, God's Power and Wisdom
(1 Corinthians 1:8–25)

SATURDAY
Know Jesus Christ Crucified
(1 Corinthians 2:1–5)

SUNDAY
Lydia, Model of Hospitality Practice
(Acts 16:11–15, 40;
1 Corinthians 1:26–30)

PREPARE FOR NEXT SUNDAY

Read **Deuteronomy 18:15-22** and next week's lesson, "Moses: Prophet of Deliverance."

Sources:
Strong, James. *The New Strong's Exhaustive Concordance of the Bible.* Nashville, TN: Thomas Nelson, 2003.
Thayer, Joseph Henry. *A Greek-English Lexicon of the New Testament.* New York: American Book Company, 1994.
Vine, W.E. *Vine's Complete Expository Dictionary of Old and New Testament Words.* Nashville, TN: Thomas Nelson, 1996.

COMMENTS / NOTES:

_____

_____

_____

_____

_____

_____

_____

_____

_____

_____

_____

_____

_____

_____

_____

_____

_____

_____

_____

_____

_____

The Symbol of the Church Of God In Christ

The Symbol of the Church Of God In Christ is an outgrowth of the Presiding Bishop's Coat of Arms, which has become quite familiar to the Church. The design of the Official Seal of the Church was created in 1973 and adopted in the General Assembly in 1981 (July Session).

The obvious GARNERED WHEAT in the center of the seal represents all of the people of the Church Of God In Christ, Inc. The ROPE of wheat that holds the shaft together represents the Founding Father of the Church, Bishop Charles Harrison Mason, who, at the call of the Lord, banded us together as a Brotherhood of Churches in the First Pentecostal General Assembly of the Church, in 1907.

The date in the seal has a two-fold purpose: first, to tell us that Bishop Mason received the baptism of the Holy Ghost in March 1907 and, second, to tell us that it was because of this outpouring that Bishop Mason was compelled to call us together in February of 1907 to organize the Church Of God In Christ.

The RAIN in the background represents the Latter Rain, or the End-time Revivals, which brought about the emergence of our Church along with other Pentecostal Holiness Bodies in the same era. The rain also serves as a challenge to the Church to keep Christ in the center of our worship and service, so that He may continue to use the Church Of God In Christ as one of the vehicles of Pentecostal Revival before the return of the Lord.

This information was reprinted from the book *So You Want to KNOW YOUR CHURCH* by Alferd Z. Hall, Jr.

COGIC AFFIRMATION OF FAITH

We believe the Bible to be the inspired and only infallible written Word of God.

We believe that there is One God, eternally existent in three Persons: God the Father, God the Son, and God the Holy Spirit.

We believe in the Blessed Hope, which is the rapture of the Church of God, which is in Christ at His return.

We believe that the only means of being cleansed from sin is through repentance and faith in the precious Blood of Jesus Christ.

We believe that regeneration by the Holy Ghost is absolutely essential for personal salvation.

We believe that the redemptive work of Christ on the Cross provides healing for the human body in answer to believing in prayer.

We believe that the baptism in the Holy Ghost, according to Acts 2:4, is given to believers who ask for it.

We believe in the sanctifying power of the Holy Spirit, by whose indwelling the Christian is enabled to live a Holy and separated life in this present world. Amen.

The Doctrines of the Church Of God In Christ

THE BIBLE

We believe that the Bible is the Word of God and contains one harmonious and sufficiently complete system of doctrine. We believe in the full inspiration of the Word of God. We hold the Word of God to be the only authority in all matters and assert that no doctrine can be true or essential if it does not find a place in this Word.

THE FATHER

We believe in God, the Father Almighty, the Author and Creator of all things. The Old Testament reveals God in diverse manners, by manifesting His nature, character, and dominions. The Gospels in the New Testament give us knowledge of God the "Father" or "My Father," showing the relationship of God to Jesus as Father, or representing Him as the Father in the Godhead, and Jesus himself that Son (St. John 15:8, 14:20). Jesus also gives God the distinction of "Fatherhood" to all believers when He explains God in the light of "Your Father in Heaven" (St. Matthew 6:8).

THE SON

We believe that Jesus Christ is the Son of God, the second person in the Godhead of the Trinity or Triune Godhead. We believe that Jesus was and is eternal in His person and nature as the Son of God who was with God in the beginning of creation (St. John 1:1). We believe that Jesus Christ was born of a virgin called Mary according to the Scripture (St. Matthew 1:18), thus giving rise to our fundamental belief in the Virgin Birth and to all of the miraculous events surrounding the phenomenon (St. Matthew 1:18–25). We believe that Jesus Christ became the "suffering servant" to man; this suffering servant came seeking to redeem man from sin and to reconcile him to God, his Father (Romans 5:10). We believe that Jesus Christ is standing now as mediator between God and man (I Timothy 2:5).

THE HOLY GHOST

We believe the Holy Ghost or Holy Spirit is the third person of the Trinity; proceeds from the Father and the Son; is of the same substance, equal to power and glory; and is together with the Father and the Son, to be believed in, obeyed, and worshiped. The Holy Ghost is a gift bestowed upon the believer for the purpose of equipping and empowering the believer, making him or her a more effective witness for service in the world. He teaches and guides one into all truth (John 16:13; Acts 1:8, 8:39).

THE BAPTISM OF THE HOLY GHOST

We believe that the Baptism of the Holy Ghost is an experience subsequent to conversion and sanctification and that tongue-speaking is the consequence of the baptism in the Holy Ghost with the manifestations of the fruit of the spirit (Galatians 5:22–23; Acts 10:46, 19:1–6). We believe that we are not baptized with the Holy Ghost in order to be saved (Acts 19:1–6; John 3:5). When one receives a baptismal Holy Ghost experience, we believe one will speak with a tongue unknown to oneself according to the sovereign will of Christ. To be filled with the Spirit means to be Spirit controlled as expressed by Paul in Ephesians 5:18,19. Since the charismatic demonstrations were necessary to help the early church to be successful in implementing the command of Christ, we, therefore, believe that a Holy Ghost experience is mandatory for all believers today.

MAN

We believe that humankind was created holy by God, composed of body, soul, and spirit. We believe that humankind, by nature, is sinful and unholy. Being born in sin, a person needs to be born again, sanctified and cleansed from all sins by the blood of Jesus. We believe that one is saved by confessing and forsaking one's sins, and believing on the Lord Jesus Christ, and that having become a child of God, by being born again and adopted into the family of God, one may, and should, claim the inheritance of the sons of God, namely the baptism of the Holy Ghost.

SIN

Sin, the Bible teaches, began in the angelic world (Ezekiel 28:11–19; Isaiah 14:12–20) and is transmitted into the blood of the human race through disobedience and deception motivated by unbelief (I Timothy 2:14). Adam's sin, committed by eating of the forbidden fruit from the tree of knowledge of good and evil, carried with it permanent pollution or depraved human nature in all his descendants. This is called "original sin." Sin can now be defined as a volitional transgression against God and a lack of conformity to the will of God. We, therefore, conclude that humankind by nature is sinful and has fallen from a glorious and righteous state from which we were created, and has become unrighteous and unholy.

We therefore, must be restored to the state of holiness from which we have fallen by being born again (St. John 3:7).

SALVATION

Salvation deals with the application of the work of redemption to the sinner with restoration to divine favor and communion with God. This redemptive operation of the Holy Ghost upon sinners is brought about by repentance toward God and faith toward our Lord Jesus Christ which brings conversion, faith, justification, regeneration, sanctification, and the baptism of the Holy Ghost. Repentance is the work of God, which results in a change of mind in respect to a person's relationship to God (St. Matthew 3:1–2, 4:17; Acts 20:21). Faith is a certain conviction wrought in the heart by the Holy Spirit, as to the truth of the Gospel and a heart trust in the promises of God in Christ (Romans 1:17, 3:28; St. Matthew 9:22; Acts 26:18). Conversion is that act of God whereby He causes the regenerated sinner, in one's conscious life, to turn to Him in repentance and faith (II Kings 5:15; II Chronicles 33:12,13; St. Luke 19:8,9; Acts 8:30). Regeneration is the act of God by which the principle of the new life is implanted in humankind, the governing disposition of soul is made holy, and the first holy exercise of this new disposition is secured. Sanctification is that gracious and continuous operation of the Holy Ghost, by which He delivers the justified sinner from the pollution of sin, renews a person's whole nature in the image of God, and enables one to perform good works (Romans 6:4, 5:6; Colossians 2:12, 3:1).

ANGELS

The Bible uses the term "angel" (a heavenly body) clearly and primarily to denote messengers or ambassadors of God with such Scripture references as Revelations 4:5, which indicates their duty in heaven to praise God (Psalm 103:20), to do God's will (St. Matthew 18:10), and to behold His face. But since heaven must come down to earth, they also have a mission to earth. The Bible indicates that they accompanied God in the Creation, and also that they will accompany Christ in His return in Glory.

DEMONS

Demons denote unclean or evil spirits; they are sometimes called devils or demonic beings. They are evil spirits, belonging to the unseen or spiritual realm, embodied in human beings. The Old Testament refers to the prince of demons, sometimes called Satan (adversary) or Devil, as having power and wisdom, taking the habitation of other forms such as the serpent (Genesis 3:1). The New Testament speaks of the Devil as Tempter (St. Matthew 4:3), and it goes on to tell the works of Satan, the Devil, and demons as combating righteousness and good in any form, proving to be an adversary to the saints. Their chief power is exercised to destroy the mission of Jesus Christ. It can well be said that the Christian Church believes in demons, Satan, and devils. We believe in their power and purpose. We believe they can be subdued and conquered as in the commandment to the believer by Jesus. "In my name they shall cast out Satan and the work of the Devil and to resist him and then he will flee (WITHDRAW) from you" (St. Mark 16:17).

THE CHURCH

The Church forms a spiritual unity of which Christ is the divine head. It is animated by one Spirit, the Spirit of Christ. It professes one faith, shares one hope, and serves one King. It is the citadel of the truth and God's agency for communicating to believers all spiritual blessings. The Church then is the object of our faith rather than of knowledge. The name of our Church, "CHURCH OF GOD IN CHRIST," is supported by I Thessalonians 2:14 and other passages in the Pauline Epistles. The word "CHURCH" or "EKKLESIA" was first applied to the Christian society by Jesus Christ in St. Matthew 16:18, the occasion being that of His benediction of Peter at Caesarea Philippi.

THE SECOND COMING OF CHRIST

We believe in the second coming of Christ; that He shall come from heaven to earth, personally, bodily, visibly (Acts 1:11; Titus 2:11–13; St. Matthew 16:27, 24:30, 25:30; Luke 21:27; John 1:14, 17; Titus 2:11); and that the Church, the bride, will be caught up to meet Him in the air (I Thessalonians 4:16–17). We admonish all who have this hope to purify themselves as He is pure.

DIVINE HEALING

The Church Of God In Christ believes in and practices Divine Healing. It is a commandment of Jesus to the Apostles (St. Mark 16:18). Jesus affirms His teachings on healing by explaining to His disciples, who were to be Apostles, that healing the afflicted is by faith (St. Luke 9:40–41). Therefore, we believe that healing by faith in God has scriptural support and ordained authority. St. James's writings in his epistle encourage Elders to pray for the sick, lay hands upon them and to anoint them with oil, and state that prayers with faith shall heal the sick and the Lord shall raise them up. Healing is still practiced widely and frequently in the Church Of God In Christ, and testimonies of healing in our Church testify to this fact.

MIRACLES

The Church Of God In Christ believes that miracles occur to convince people that the Bible is God's Word. A miracle can be defined as an extraordinary visible act of divine power, wrought by the efficient agency of the will of God, which has as its final cause the vindication of the righteousness of God's Word. We believe that the works of God, which were performed during the beginnings of Christianity, do and will occur even today where God is preached, faith in Christ is exercised, the Holy Ghost is active, and the Gospel is promulgated in the truth (Acts 5:15, 6:8, 9:40; Luke 4:36, 7:14, 15, 5:5, 6; St. Mark 14:15).

THE ORDINANCES OF THE CHURCH

It is generally admitted that for an ordinance to be valid, it must have been instituted by Christ. When we speak of ordinances of the church, we are speaking of those instituted by Christ, in which by sensible signs the grace of God in Christ and the benefits of the covenant of grace are represented, sealed, and applied to believers, and these in turn give expression to their faith and allegiance to God. The Church Of God In Christ recognizes three ordinances as having been instituted by Christ himself and, therefore, are binding upon the church practice.

THE LORD'S SUPPER (HOLY COMMUNION)

The Lord's Supper symbolizes the Lord's death and suffering for the benefit and in the place of His people. It also symbolizes the believer's participation in the crucified Christ. It represents not only the death of Christ as the object of faith, which unites the believers to Christ, but also the effect of this act as the giving of life, strength, and joy to the soul. The communicant by faith enters into a special spiritual union of one's soul with the glorified Christ.

FOOT WASHING

Foot washing is practiced and recognized as an ordinance in our Church because Christ, by His example, showed that humility characterized greatness in the kingdom of God, and that service rendered to others gave evidence that humility, motivated by love, exists. These services are held subsequent to the Lord's Supper; however, its regularity is left to the discretion of the pastor in charge.

WATER BAPTISM

We believe that Water Baptism is necessary as instructed by Christ in St. John 3:5, "UNLESS MAN BE BORN AGAIN OF WATER AND OF THE SPIRIT..."

However, we do not believe that water baptism alone is a means of salvation, but is an outward demonstration that one has already had a conversion experience and has accepted Christ as his personal Savior. As Pentecostals, we practice immersion in preference to sprinkling because immersion corresponds more closely to the death, burial, and resurrection of our Lord (Colossians 2:12). It also symbolizes regeneration and purification more than any other mode. Therefore, we practice immersion as our mode of baptism. We believe that we should use the Baptismal Formula given to us by Christ for all "...IN THE NAME OF THE FATHER, AND OF THE SON, AND OF THE HOLY GHOST..." (Matthew 28:19).

Call to order.
Singing.
Prayer.
Responsive reading:

t.: Behold, how good and how pleasant it is for brethren to dwell together in unity!

Psalm 133:1

ool: And let the peace of God rule in your hearts, to the which also ye are called in one body; and be ye thankful.

Colossians 3:15

t.: Blessed are they that dwell in thy house: they will be still praising thee.

Psalm 84:4

ool: Praise ye the LORD. I will praise the LORD with my whole heart, in the assembly of the upright, and in the congregation.

Psalm 111:1

t.: And the LORD said unto him, I have heard thy prayer and thy supplication, that thou hast made before me: I have hallowed this house, which thou hast built, to put my name there for ever; and mine eyes and mine heart shall be there perpetually.

1 Kings 9:3

ool: Ye shall keep my sabbaths, and reverence my sanctuary: I am the LORD.

Leviticus 19:30

Supt.: And I say also unto thee, That thou art Peter, and upon this rock I will build my church; and the gates of hell shall not prevail against it.

Matthew 16:18

School: My soul longeth, yea, even fainteth for the courts of the LORD: my heart and my flesh crieth out for the living God.

Psalm 84:2

Supt.: And other sheep I have, which are not of this fold: them also I must bring, and they shall hear my voice; and there shall be one fold, and one shepherd.

John 10:16

School: But if I tarry long, that thou mayest know how thou oughtest to behave thyself in the house of God, which is the church of the living God, the pillar and ground of the truth.

1 Timothy 3:15

All: Lift up your hands in the sanctuary, and bless the LORD.

Psalm 134:2

5. Singing.
6. Reading lesson by school and superintendent.
7. Classes assemble for lesson study.
8. Sunday School offering.
9. Five-minute warning bell.
10. Closing bell.
11. Brief lesson review by pastor or superintendent.
12. Secretary's report.
13. Announcements.
14. Dismissal.

NOTES

ONPASSIVE.COM